TOO COLD FOR ALLIGATORS

Other books by Sasha Wolfe:

My Life Isn't Flowers: Poetry, art work and photography

Through the Window: in, around, and reflections there of

Two poetry chapbooks:
They Will Never Write Songs about Me
Dancing with Butterflies

New upcoming books:
Random Day Trips

TOO COLD FOR ALLIGATORS

Thirty-Three Days on the Road

Sasha Wolfe

Artist, Photographer, Writer

Maps drawn by Nan McCarthy of
Nan McCarthy Impeccably Detailed Fine Art

authorHOUSE®

AuthorHouse™ LLC
1663 Liberty Drive
Bloomington, IN 47403
www.authorhouse.com
Phone: 1-800-839-8640

www.sashawolfe.net
sashawo@tds.net

All photographs are by Sasha Wolfe.
All maps drawn by Nan McCarthy.

Published by AuthorHouse 08/06/2014

ISBN: 978-1-4969-2338-7 (sc)
ISBN: 978-1-4969-2337-0 (e)

DISCLAIMER: The bits of history (all in italics) are gathered and blended from tour guides'
tales, story boards at sites, historical signs, brochures, personal stories, and various websites.
Fitting hundreds of years of history into a paragraph or two is not easy. I tried to research various
bridges and was able to find information on some, but not others. Forgive me for any errors.

This book is printed on acid-free paper.

CONTENTS

PHOTOS

MAPS

DEDICATION

To my mother, Marge Brewster, who supported me in all things even when we did not agree. She was often highly critical, but she always believed in me and wanted the best for me. She was so proud of my artistic abilities.

She would have totally supported me on taking this great adventure and it's thanks to her that this trip is possible. I owe her so much.

Thank-you, Ma, wherever you are.
I miss you so much.
I love you.
I will always love you.

ACKNOWLEDGMENTS

I am very grateful to my family, friends and neighbors for their support and encouragement. Without their kind words and enthusiasm that I do this, courage would have failed me and the dream would have remained just that . . . a dream.

And so, heartfelt thanks go to:

My mother – even though she is no longer physically here, made it possible for me to afford this. She would have been so proud of me and would have been eager for my return to hear my stories.

My sons, Eric Fowler and Adam Fowler; their wives, Sophia and Michelle; my brother and his wife, Don and Carol Brewster – were all for me going, knowing that I had to go away for awhile and for giving me their understanding and love.

Gail Sawyer – my first-ever friend and chosen sister; although separated in childhood with time and distance keeping us out of touch for many years, our connection remained and was strongly rekindled when she returned "home." Without Gail's own journey and conviction to do winter in the south, I would not have dared to undertake my own. Her encouragement and support are priceless.

Nan McCarthy – dear friend and artist-sister-in-soul, encourages me in my art and gives a boost when I'm down. We have the most wonderful conversations. I treasure her advice, artist's input, and our daily e-mails are precious. I so appreciate her drawing maps for the chapters, proof reading the text, and giving valuable insight throughout the entire process.

Karen Hambleton, my wonderful neighbor – whose offer to take care of my phenomenal cat, Freyja, and keep an eye on the house, also made it possible for me to go on this extended trip. She went above and beyond and for that I cannot ever thank her enough.

Annette Vogel – owner and publisher of the *InterTown Record*, good friend and best boss I've ever had, who gave me the most wonderful job, one I can do from home or when I am on the road. Her graciousness and support pushes me to believe in myself. Through my work with her, my writing skills constantly improve.

Bob Lint and Jane Pinel – fellow artists, gallery owners, and Wednesday morning breakfast companions gave me great information on travel routes and places to visit. Bob also provided a story about mining.

Karen Winterholer – another good friend, fellow photographer, artist, and Wednesday morning breakfast companion. She took the photo of me for the back cover and provided a mining story for Day 2.

And to Gayle Hedrington – who took time from her own adventure to hunt me down when we happened to be in Savannah, Georgia on the same day. What fun to take in a favorite photography subject for both of us – trains.

My apologies for not being able to name everyone who gave great advice, suggestions, and feedback.

Thank-you, everyone, for your kindness.
Thank-you for the feedback through Facebook
and e-mails while I journeyed
and for the warm welcomes when I returned.

SASHA'S DRIVING RULES

1.) Don't set concrete plans. Be spontaneous. Allow for detours and side trips.

2.) Don't turn around or back track.
Exceptions: Unless there's something screaming to be photographed and you can't slow down in time.
The road becomes too narrow and treacherous to continue or is a dead end.
Or you change your mind.

3.) Avoid the interstates and major highways.
Exceptions: The interstates will get you to a destination sooner and sometimes great scenery can be seen from the highways.
Sometimes roads will merge with the interstates for a distance.

4.) Use maps and atlases only to get a general idea of places to visit before you leave.
Exceptions: It's okay to use them for a quick referral if you stop for something else.
It's okay to use them after the journey to go over your route and help you remember.

5.) It is not necessary to do each trip the same way. Go with the moment, with what catches your attention.

6.) Stop at historical markers: take photographs of those and site storyboards to research info later.

7.) Don't be afraid to talk to people. Most would love to tell you a story.

8.) Stop for a meal. Choose a local restaurant that gets a lot of business. Exception: It's okay to stop at a chain restaurant if you really like the food. No fast food chains unless you're desperate.

9.) Be satisfied with the day's accomplishments. You can't do everything in one day. It's okay to return to a place on another day if you feel you missed something or you want to explore more.

10.) It's okay to do research after the journey for history and other town information.

INTRODUCTION

An Idea Forms

Gail went to Florida for the winter stopping along the way to visit with family and friends. I envy her adventure. On her return north, she talks about spending the next winter in Florida. A light bulb goes off in my head. Why couldn't I do that?

Once voiced, we begin chatting like magpies about the possibilities. She and her dad will be renting a place in Jensen Beach. I can justify the trip with the excuse to visit them, do my newspaper editing work on my laptop as most hotels will have Wi-Fi, and also write about the journey. I've always wanted to drive across county, taking time to see sights without worrying about a time frame. While this journey won't be totally across country, traveling from New Hampshire to Florida would certainly be an adventure of a lifetime, especially as I'll be traveling alone.

Excitement fills me, but knowing myself, I am not sure if the trip will come to fruition. I tend to make many plans and most fall by the wayside. As the weeks go by, I talk about the possibility to others. Everyone agrees it would be a great thing to do and I know if I keep talking about it, they will push me to go.

Planning and Preparation

Months go into planning. The first purchase is a 2013 Road Atlas and hours and days are spent perusing possible routes. Between sites on the maps, suggestions from friends, and visiting websites, I am finding so many interesting places that I wonder if I will make it TO Florida. The second purchase is a cell phone and not having service at the house, there are problems from the beginning. After wasting a month of fees, I am finally told by Verizon to wait until the first night in a hotel before reactivating.

Throughout the months of planning, my mind runs wild. Sometimes the chatter is so bad I am almost in a state of panic. Do I really have the courage to travel alone? I am petrified of cities and crowds; I don't like driving on the freeways and have trouble talking to strangers. Plus, there are concerns about winter weather. How far south will I need to go before finding warmer temperatures?

My mind flips to the other side and excitement fills me. I love being spontaneous! I plan basic routes, but leave myself open to changes. If I like an area, I may choose to stay more than one day. That means hotels are not booked ahead of time. How can I know where I will be on any given night? Some decisions won't be made until I am in the area. Will I go through Gettysburg or stay on I-81? Will I do the Skyline Drive or head towards the coast?

Not only am I encouraged by family and friends, but something inside tells me I have to do this. The past years spent with my mother were very difficult as I watched her decline. My world narrowed in 2006 after I quit working full time to stay home with her. While it had its upside in that I was able to be a full time artist as well as her care giver, it got harder and harder to leave the house. The year following her death was filled with ups and downs as I dealt with the grief of losing her and work at becoming a successful artist. It got so I didn't want to leave the house at all. By year's end, with the upcoming anniversary of her passing (Christmas day 2011) and receiving devastating negative comments on some of my art work, I had a total meltdown.

I need this trip for my own well-being and sanity. I haven't been on a vacation in over 10 years, not even an overnight trip. The more I stay home, the harder it is to go anywhere. It's time to get away for awhile and find a new lease on life.

SUNDAY, JANUARY 20

The Day Before: Leaving and Coming Home

It's down to the wire. If I can get the house relatively clean today, I shall leave tomorrow. What does that mean to me mentally? This trip has been in the planning for months, and as much as I want to do it, there was always the chance that I would back out. Now, the time has arrived, and while there is much excitement, there is also much trepidation. I'm scared, excited, and my emotions are running wild.

Why would I think about backing out? Fear . . . fear of the unknown, crowds, cities, PEOPLE. I am basically a very shy person. It takes a lot of courage for me to speak to someone unless I know them well. You might not think that from the way I write, but it is extremely hard for me to attend functions, do interviews, or even go out to dinner. Sometimes even when I know the people, it is difficult to approach them.

Strangers in unfamiliar territories are going to test me to the limit, but this will be good. I tend to avoid trying new things especially if I think there might be a lot of people around. I want to push myself. I want to be better around people. As an artist wanting to sell my work, it is important to be comfortable around potential customers. As writer and photo-journalist for the local newspaper, it is necessary to be at ease with people so they will tell me stories.

I am eager to see scenery, natural settings, and historical sites. Yes, there will be people around, but the pictures in my mind are not showing CROWDS. I will feel safe. It's not that I'm afraid of being mugged or anything like that. That's the farthest from my mind. Oh, how do I explain this?

I suppose it all goes back to my childhood when I was ridiculed all through school. I had few friends. That's probably why I fear people. It's about wanting to be accepted. I want people to like me. I'm not afraid of physical hurt, but emotional hurt. Does that make sense? There's being alone, which

I don't mind as I like solitude, and there's being ALONE, which is about being lonely. I can be happy by myself, but alone amongst others makes me feel isolated and shunned.

So, now that it is time to leave, my fears are escalating. The thought of leaving Freyja behind and how lonely she will be makes me cry. Karen will take excellent care of my precious puss, but my baby will miss me and I will miss her. It breaks my heart to think about it.

Then there will be the coming home. Years ago when on vacation, I hated coming home. I hated the thought of going back to a job in the corporate world. It's different now. I live alone except for Freyja. I am living the life of an artist. What more could I want? (Okay, maybe more sales.) I love where I live; it's a great community, I have friends, and I love my job with the paper. So, what's the problem?

The house doesn't feel mine. It doesn't feel like a forever home. It's just a place I live and there are too many reminders of my mother. If it wasn't for Freyja, I wouldn't care if I didn't come back. I am hoping this trip will help me get my head on straight. I want to reevaluate myself as an artist and determine where to go from here. I need to decide whether to keep the house or sell. (I hate moving, hate dealing with real estate and all the legal crap and complications, but I do want a house that will be mine and fit my lifestyle.)

The excitement is stronger than the fear; I am going to have a most awesome adventure!

PART 1

THE JOURNEY SOUTH

Who am I at the leaving and who will I be when I return?

You're Going Away?

DAY 1, MONDAY, JANUARY 21

Hitting the Road

It's a beautiful day to be out and about, although frigid. I could have crawled out of bed at 4:30, but the room was cold. I force myself up at 5 a.m., check computer messages and write in the journal. I'm just about all packed with the truck loaded . . . or so I thought. Good thing the check list was reviewed. I would have forgotten the road atlas. CDs and CD player are also added because the player on the laptop makes noise. A set of pastels go in the bag with the charcoal drawing supplies. Phone calls were made yesterday to family and the police chief. As soon as this writing is done, the laptop will go in its bag and I will hit the road. How exciting this all is! The goal for today is to take Rte. 9 through Vermont. I don't know how many times I'll have to stop for a break or photographs. Who knows where I'll be tonight.

I don't see Freyja when I go out the door, but holler my usual goodbye. The door is locked at 9 a.m. It is 19 degrees, the air is brisk and clear and the skies blue with a few gray puffy clouds. The odometer reads 13,166.1. It suddenly hits that I'm actually leaving HOME! My eyes fill with tears. The leaving is quite emotional. My vision blurs as I drive down the road. One bad thing about traveling alone is that I only have my own thoughts and no one to talk to or distract me. I cry for Freyja. Already I miss her and the thought of her missing me and not understanding that I will return creates a sharp lump in my throat. I can't drive and cry. I've got to pull myself together. Karen will take good care of my kitty.

First stop is in Hillsborough for gas; $3.34/gal. I have not driven towards Keene very often and those times were summer, so the scenery is very different. The snow on the rocks in the brooks reminds me of puffy capes draped over shoulders; a stark whiteness to the darker stone and water below. I want to stop for photos, but keep going. There's always regret at not stopping. I always think I'll come back on another day, but I seldom do. Today I am eager to get away from the cold. How far south will I have to get before I leave these frigid temperatures behind?

Crossing into Vermont

A stop is made on the side of the road before the bridge that spans the Connecticut River. The time is 10:30, the odometer is at 13,228.3, and it is 24 degrees. Vermont has a seat belt law, so after taking a couple photos out the windshield, I reach for the seat belt. It stops before it reaches the buckle. Oh, no! Have I gained that much weight? It's not like I've never worn the belt. What am I going to do?

I drive across the bridge into Brattleboro holding the belt across me with one hand to find a safer place to stop. This is new territory. I've been as far as the bridge before, but never crossed it. My thoughts are stampeding and I am freaking. Will I get pulled over and ticketed? What's going on with the belt?

As I come up to a rotary at the intersection of Rtes. 5 and 9, there is a Friendly's off to the far left. That would be a good place to get off the road and have breakfast. I pull out onto the rotary. This stupid seatbelt is distracting me as I try to hold it across my lap and figure out where to go. I also keep an eye out for Rte. 9W. There are cars behind me, in front of me, and on the rotary itself.

Suddenly, there's a car inches away from the driver's side window. A silent scream of shock shatters my mind and my heart jumps into my throat. Where did that come from? I swear I looked. I freeze waiting for the crunch, but it doesn't happen. There are no blaring horns or squealing tires which makes it even more bizarre. The woman zips in front of me taking the exit on the right. My heart pounds, hands shake, and I want to burst into tears. I don't know how we didn't collide and it would have been my fault. I continue slowly around the rotary feeling sick to my stomach and pull into Friendly's. What a way to begin the journey in a new state.

I'm too rattled to eat, but off the road and out of traffic, I calm down and can think clearly. I am short and the seat is pulled up close to the steering wheel. Also, the seat back is straight which is better for my back. Both of these situations require more seatbelt length. The Owner's Manual mentions height adjustments and seatbelt extension and I raise the adjustment, take off my coat, and snap, the belt connects. Whew. Unfortunately, the strap comes down the left side of my neck and across my throat. If I get in an accident, I will be strangled or have my throat slit.

It's one way out of the parking lot which means back around the rotary – which I do very cautiously. To continue on Rte. 9W, I-91S is taken for a short distance to the next exit. Oh, this is a much enjoyable drive along narrow, curvy country roads passing through quaint villages. Traffic is almost non-existent. Derelict buildings with the snowy backdrops dot the landscape. I kick myself for not stopping; again telling myself I will come back some other time. What a beautiful drive. Farms, fields, forests, and brooks are passed; lovely country. The road goes up and up and up with many twists and turns. I begin seeing signs stating, "Molly Stark Trail."

Short History Lesson

Molly Stark was born Elizabeth Page. Her father, Caleb Page, was the first postmaster in New Hampshire. They lived in Dunbarton. Molly married General John Stark who was famous for the Battle of Bennington in Vermont during the war for American Independence. Molly earned fame for being a nurse to many of Stark's troops. What is now Rte. 9 could possibly have been the route that Stark and his troops took on the way home from the battle. John Stark, in later years, coined the phrase "Live Free or Die" which eventually became New Hampshire's state motto.

I want to look around more, but eyes need to stay on the road. A quick stop is made for photos on Hogback Mountain, but it's too cold and windy to get out of the truck. As breathtaking as the view is, it's still winter and the scene is dull and bluish.

Rte. 9 passes through the Green Mountains and eventually winds down and down coming into Bennington. Do I stay on Rte. 9 which looks to go right through the city or follow signs for Troy, N.Y. which will put me on Rte. 279? Uh, oh, I hadn't looked at the map that closely. Rte. 279 looks like a by-pass and I take that hoping I'm going the right way knowing I have to go to Troy. It seems a long way around and Vermont Rte. 7 merges for a bit before taking its journey north. Rte. 279 crosses the Walloomsac River and on into New York where it merges onto N.Y. 7 in Hoosick.

Getting Through New York Takes Forever

There is less snow in New York with only speckles in the fields. Trees give way to more open landscape and beautiful farm lands. Miles of huge rolling hills and crooked fences break up the emptiness. Oh, why don't I stop? I love the big farms. Traffic slows, bunches up, and becomes bumper to bumper, stop and go for miles. Full attention is needed on the driving. There are so many places that would make great photos, but no safe place to pull over in this traffic. In Hoosick Center, there is one small set of lights. This is the hold up? There's nothing here. At least past the lights, speed picks up to 55 mph. The Hoosick River is crossed.

I break for lunch at 12:40 p.m. at the Country View Diner in Brunswick, N.Y. where I am seated next to a family with loud talking kids. It's rude to put single people next to kids. Is it because I'm a woman and people automatically assume women like to be around children? I prefer quiet. The high voices and constant antics make me very uncomfortable and I only eat half my sandwich. Back in the truck, the struggle with the seatbelt resumes. I work myself into a frustrated sweat. I can't see what I'm doing and rely on feel. This is so aggravating. The coat was already removed and now I take off the sweater. It works. Maybe I've been holding the buckle at the wrong angle. Thank heavens the heater kicks in quickly.

The traffic is again bumper to bumper. Heading into Troy, I have to find Rte. 87, the New York State Thruway south. I should have looked at the map when I stopped. The heavy traffic is nerve wracking and not knowing which lane to be in doubles the stress. There is a division with Rte. 7W bearing left and Rte. 787 to the right. The sign saying Albany points right. South should be left, but I know I have to go through Albany. Do I take Rte. 7 into downtown Troy and hope it takes me to the thruway? I don't dare glance at the map while watching the stop-and-go traffic. This is scary. I take the right hoping that Rte. 787 is a by-pass of the downtown area.

I continue driving west not sure I'm on the right road. The Hudson River is crossed, but little is noticed as I'm worried about the road and the traffic. Rte. 787 makes a long loop around to turn south and follows the Hudson River into Albany where it turns westward. Finally signs appear for the thruway.

The New York State Thruway was built in the mid 1950s and is considered the fifth busiest toll road in the U.S. Its mainline is 496 miles between the Pennsylvania border at Ripley and the Garden State Parkway connector at the border of New Jersey. The entire route with its six individual components connects four states and Ontario, Canada for a total of 569.8 miles.

In New Hampshire, the toll booths have signs saying EZ Pass or Cash. Here there are signs that say EZ Pass Only and one solitary booth with a single green light. This is confusing. I guess at the green light and I'm given a card and told to pay at the end. It is 82 miles to Interstate 84. The speed limit is 65, but few vehicles go that . . . slow. My speed averages about 75; faster than I normally drive. I don't know when the sky clouded over, but it's darker and overcast. More cars have headlights on than not. It feels like everyone in the world is heading towards New York City. There's not much chance to look around, but the farmlands and the huge silos along the rolling hills are amazing. There are a lot of hawks. My feet and legs ache. The new sneakers are tight. This is taking forever. I'm bored and begin to doubt making Pennsylvania today.

Finally, the sign for I-84 is seen and what a convoluted-turn-around set of ramps from one highway to the next. This is a trip unto itself! As it is so often, ramps seem to go around in a circle . . . and around. I cross over I-84 continuing south until the exit ramp which curves in a long arc to the right coming around to pass over the thruway. Then after a straight stretch, the ramp makes a gradual turn left making me feel I am back on the thruway heading north again. In the meantime, there are multiple on and off ramps. I follow the signs for I-84W and another curve left crossing over the interstate again.

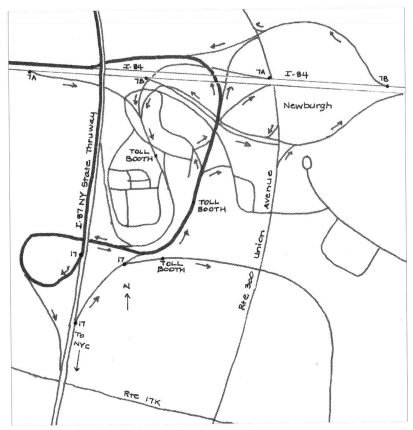

Feels a lot more convoluted than the map shows.

After over one mile of ramp, I come to the toll booths. The EZ Pass ones are clearly marked. This time there are two with a single green light each on either side of the six-booth EZ Pass strip. I head for the one on the far right. What if I'm wrong? What would happen if I am in a wrong lane? I pull up not knowing how much it will cost. I certainly couldn't stop in traffic to read the tiny print on the ticket. Thankfully, no one is behind me as $3.85 is fumbled out of the cup holders. With the seat belt on, I can't access my pockets.

Pulling away from the toll booth, a moment of panic sets in as I see the sign for I-84W on the far left of the ramp. Oh, my, gosh, I have to cross eight lanes! Luckily, for the first time since being in New York there isn't any traffic. Good thing as another near accident might put me over the edge. This ramp also winds round and round and up over freeway and although the sign said I-84W, I feel like I am going around in a circle and headed back north on the thruway again. I am so glad to see another sign saying I-84W.

My mind is reeling from that confusing ramp. It takes awhile of straight highway driving before my heart stops pounding. The road surface is rough. The speed limit is 55. My average is 70 as I keep up with the Joneses. I see my first dead deer in the median, begin counting the exits down; 5E, 4, 3, 2, and debate about going into Pennsylvania. By this time, the pain in my legs and feet are adding to the stress of the highway driving, so when I see a Days Inn sign at Exit 1, I figure this is it, I'm done for the day.

First Night Away from Home

This is Port Jervis, N.Y. where the Delaware and Neversink Rivers merge. The ramp comes down from the highway and three lefts are taken to pass under the highway and climb a road to the entrance of the Days Inn which is almost parallel to the highway. Port Jervis is just north of the New Jersey border and Pennsylvania is across the river to the west. The odometer reads 13,434.8 for a daily total of 268.7 miles.

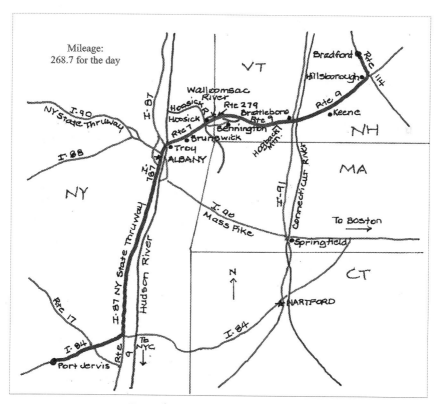

From home to Port Jervis, N.Y.

9

The guy at the desk is very nice explaining how to access the internet. This is my first time using the computer away from home. He lets me use a luggage trolley. I'm in the last room down and can access the hallway from the door at the end. Things needed for the night are hauled in. It's snowing. I'm starving and check the brochures for delivery. Ewww, BBQ Chinese? I don't think so. I order a cheese pizza.

The room is disappointing. The more I look around, the more my stomach churns. The bedspread and chairs have big ugly stains. There's dust and cobwebs on the ceilings. It doesn't seem like this room has been used in awhile. I don't even want to mention the bathroom.

I set up the laptop and while it is firing up, plug in the CD player and put in the Moody Blues. The heater is turned on. It's horribly noisy and rattles. There's no problem getting internet access and soon I'm checking messages and writing my blog. Karen reports that she did not see Freyja, but kitty is eating and using the litter box. I call Verizon Wireless to activate the cell phone then call my brother, Don, to let him know where I am for the night. The television only has four channels, none clear and nothing I want to watch. I chat on Facebook with Gail, Gayle, and Annie. Being able to have these contacts makes me feel that I'm not alone.

My goal for the day was accomplished. I wanted to get through Vermont and New York. I did. However, I am a little disappointed. Why do I think I should only take pictures when I get south of West Virginia? Why don't I stop other places? No, it would not be smart to stop along the big highways, but there are places where I could have taken the time. This isn't anything new. It's a habit. Many opportunities are presented and I just don't take the time.

Well, part of the idea for this trip is to stop and take the time. I am surprised that more stops weren't needed because of my leg. I do want to stop more often, though. I will tomorrow. Pennsylvania will not just be a drive through.

I call it a night at 9:30 and crawl into that questionable bed. At least the sheets look clean. I fall asleep listening to the highway whine and the heater rattle.

DAY 2, TUESDAY, JANUARY 22

Seat belt Fight

It's a sleepless night. The hot air blowing from the noisy heater is not quite loud enough to drown out highway traffic. The air is very dry. I am out of bed by 5 a.m. with a bad headache. In the light of day, there's more of an impression this room hasn't been used for awhile. The stains on the bed covering and chair are more pronounced. Really eww! Haven't these people heard of stain remover? I am afraid to sit on the bed to get dressed. There are cobwebs and dust hanging from the ceiling. I don't even want to look close at the black specks in the grout and caulking in the shower. The coffee cup leaks while I am cleaning up and spreads out over the table. The Verizon cell phone paperwork is ruined. What a mess. Thankfully, the paper soaks up the liquid before it reaches the laptop. The coffee is horrible anyway. I get out my stainless travel mug and the next cup of coffee goes into that. I miss the Keurig.

Messages are checked on the laptop and the morning journal writing takes until 7 a.m. The hotel invoice was slipped under the door during the night. At check-in, I was given a price of $69.95. Now I find other charges; $5.77 for state tax and $3.50 for local tax making the total for one night, $79.22. Why can't people say the real total when giving the price? Do customers care how much goes to taxes? I am only interested in what I have to pay and it's depressing to find extra charges.

It's 9 a.m. and 16 degrees when I leave the Days Inn. Coat and sweater come off before getting into the driver's seat and after a couple of attempts at the seat belt I leave it undone and drive to the bottom of the hill to the gas station. Maybe someone there can tell me where to get an extender. The station is full service (not many of them anymore) and I'm glad to not have to get out and pump gas in these cold temperatures. The price is $3.43/gal. He tells me there's an Auto Zone off the next exit, Exit 1 in Pennsylvania.

I leave the gas station frustrated. I can't get the seat belt done up at all. What the heck am I doing wrong? Getting on I-84W, the Neversink and Delaware Rivers are crossed and the ramp to Exit 1 brings me to a busy section of Matamoras, Pennsylvania. Three stores are visited and more than an hour is wasted before I give up and get back on the highway. I did manage to get the belt done up with both sweater and coat removed. The weather is dreary and cold. The windshield fills with salt and dirt as I make my way south. I should have picked up windshield washer fluid at one of the stores. At this rate, the fluid reservoirs will empty soon.

Through Scranton and Wilkes-Barre

The highway meanders west towards Scranton past farmlands similar to those in New York and climbs upwards to the Allegheny Mountains which stretch through the state. To get to Interstate 81S, I-84 turns south to merge with Rte. 380N, making a big V. It's strange to go south then go so far north to go south again, but it's the quickest and easiest way. The road surface is rougher and the ramp to I-81S loops around in a big arc and I am heading south.

Driving through Scranton is scary. The highway is above the regular city streets, and in a couple places are high walls; a kind of protective barrier, I guess. It makes me feel claustrophobic and with traffic on both sides, I really feel hemmed in. I was warned that I-81 is a big truck route, but the big trucks are not intimidating at all. However, it saddens me to not be able to look around. In those sections with the huge walls, there's nothing to see anyway.

A huge Steam Town USA sign is passed. Would that be about trains? I love trains! Should I go? How far is it? Is it in the heart of the city where I'll really be afraid and feel crowded? And it's so cold. My mind babbles. Cities freak me out. I don't dare leave the highway and soon there are signs saying "Double fines in work areas" and "Double fines over 55." No one pays attention. Focus has to be devoted to the road and though the traffic isn't horrible, I'm afraid of ending up in a wrong lane and taking an exit that will get me lost. Not that I'm afraid of getting lost. I know I'll always come out somewhere. Lost for me is ending up in a big city downtown area like New York City or Boston.

Beyond Scranton there are passes through huge rock formations. Wow, the work that must have gone into making these highways. It's amazing. I wish I could stop and take notes and pictures. I pass through Wilkes-Barre around 11:30 not even remembering the city. I am already tired from the stress and deep concentration of driving, plus I'm hungry. Off to the right an old derelict factory catches my eye. Just the kind of place I like to photograph; caving in with most the windows gone. Hmmm, maybe it's time for a break.

The next exit turns out to be just an on ramp to another highway. Oh, no! I have no idea where this goes. It throws me for a loop and for a moment, I get a little panicky and take the first exit staying to the right hoping to get back to I-81. A sign says Hanover Township. (I've noticed that a lot of Pennsylvania towns are called townships.) This back city street goes right by that factory. How lucky is that! There are row houses on the right. I'm leery about parking in front of someone's house, but I pull over and get out. I hurry around to the passenger side to put on coat and sweater as it is only12 degrees, grab the camera and head across the street.

A 10-foot tall black iron fence runs around the property preventing access. I stick the camera through the bars to get some photos. Something crunches in the barrel when focusing and now it won't move at all. Oh no! Drat, drat! I change the setting to auto focus and that works. Whew, that would be horrible to have the camera break, especially as I didn't bring a spare lens.

A huge, faded blue sign on one of the buildings says, "Blue Coal Mining," or something like that. I won't be able to tell until the picture is cropped and on a bigger screen. In a cleared area in the foreground is a newer sign saying, "Future Site of Miners Memorial." I copy down the website to research later. This must have been a coal mining facility. I don't know anything about coal mining except that it has to be a horrific job. Can you imagine going down in those mines? Were these houses across the road once homes to miners? I snap many pictures of the dilapidated buildings before the cold gets too much and I retreat to the truck. Coat and sweater come off with a lot of snapping static.

A History Lesson

Gathered from information taken off the signs, I find out the following:

This property in Ashley, Pa. was built in 1939 and later named the Huber Breaker. The facility was the largest and last remaining breaker of its time. It was able to process anthracite coal from several collieries. A colliery is a coal mine and its buildings. Blue coal, which was the name on one of the signs, is anthracite that's been sprayed with a blue iridescent chemical to keep the dust levels down.

Huber Breaker included six Menzies Cones which were used for separating coal from culm (mining refuse) by circulating high-pressure water at a rate of 8,000 gallons per minute. Seven thousand tons of coal could be processed daily. The structure incorporated huge amounts of window glass for daylight use and tar-coated sheet metal which preserved the buildings. It closed in 1976. Its architectural and technological advances are why the buildings have survived in spite of neglect and vandalism.

There are plans to turn this site into the Huber Breaker Northern Anthracite Coal Field Miner's Memorial Park which will include walking trails through landscaped scenery, benches for relaxing, and educational kiosks with information on the history of the breaker and the Anthracite Coal Region.

My friend, Bob Lint, who grew up in Pennsylvania, said there were big mines with nine-foot veins and below that four-foot veins. He worked one summer in his grandfather's mine which had a two-foot vein. He had to lie down and crawl in the shaft to dig out chunks of bituminous, or soft, coal. The chunks would then be pushed down the length of his body to his feet where another guy would pick up the pieces. Coal is very dusty and back then there were no dust masks or respirators. By the end of the day, the workers were covered head to toe with the black powder.

Bob showered every night before bed and in the morning, his pillow would be covered in black where he aspirated the dust he'd breathed in day the before. He said no matter how much he washed, that black dust just seeped out of his pores. Needless to say, he soon realized that being a coal miner was not for him. It was a scary, horrible experience.

Karen Winterholer, who was also from Pennsylvania, said that her grandfather died from black lung disease. A friend of hers offered this story: In 1959 at the Knox Mine, near Pittston, the Susquehanna River broke through the walls of the mine and rushed through killing 12 miners; some were her friends' relatives. She and her father watched from the other side the river as the engineers floated box cars into the gaping hole, thinking they could block up the gash and prevent the water from gushing in; but the mines were too cavernous and the effort was to no avail.

Karen's friend went on to say, "About six months, maybe a year later, my friend's father was driving past our house, which was just one block from the river on the other side from the disaster area, when he heard a thud behind him. As he looked back, a hole had opened up down to the mines. Two days later, the lady two doors down opened her cellar door and found the basement gone; she was looking into the mines. Their house was condemned. So, for a year, we had heavy machinery in our backyard drilling holes into which gravel was poured in vain hopes of filling the mines. I also remember my Aunt Helen saying that she could hear the miners talking when she was in her basement; that's how close they were."

Back on the Road

It's time to find my way back to I-81. I drive and drive through low-end residential areas with a few corner stores. I'm lost, but getting lost is part of the adventure. Yes, I could pull over, get out my cell phone and access GPS, but I like the challenge even though it's scary. At least this doesn't feel like a big city though my guess is this could be a suburb of Wilkes-Barre. I finally stop at a gas station to ask directions and following his advice, I come to a section of stores and restaurants seen earlier from the highway. This is great as I'm hungry.

Perkins Family Restaurant serves breakfast all day. I order the special consisting of three pancakes covered in strawberries and blackberries, two eggs, home fries, and two slices of bacon. The eggs are cooked perfectly. I don't eat eggs that often because I like them over hard with the yolks broken and they seldom arrive at the table that way. I am a little leery about something called Pancake Syrup. Is that like real maple syrup back home? I don't need it anyway with the fruit which turns out to be sweet and syrupy and not fresh. Still, the meal is tasty and filling. I can't eat it all.

On to Martinsburg, West Virginia

Back on the highway, the speed limit fluctuates between 55 and 65. Away from the city and with lesser traffic, I try to look around. There are a lot of bare spots like trees have been cut or thinned. There is one big snow-covered hill with the bare trees sticking straight up like a bunch of plain poles on a white background. The only trees that appear to have branches are the ones along the top ridge. It looks really weird, like there's something wrong. In other places the ground looks all dug up and messy. It makes me feel uncomfortable as if something terrible happened here. There are miles of this . . . ugliness. It's disturbing and unnatural. I wonder if it has something to do with mining. It isn't pretty. I can't wait to get through this area.

The highway climbs and the ugly scenery gives way to more openness. The road is cut into the side of the mountains. On one side is the rock rising so high I can't see the top from inside the truck. I chance a look to the other side and the views drop way down; miles and miles across flat valleys and then up more mountains in the far distance. I can't even guess at the distance; feet, yards, miles . . . hundreds? The road goes up and around a corner and a different vista is presented. Oh, to be able to stop, but there are no pull offs on this highway.

Then it's down, down, down. Traffic ebbs and flows. I keep looking at the thermometer in the truck waiting for the outside temperature to rise the further south I travel. It gets as low as 10 and as high as 20 degrees, but still very cold. Twenty miles before Harrisburg there isn't any more snow and the scenery changes to farmland with rolling hills and beautiful, huge farms with gigantic silos. Acres and acres of open country dotted with fences and homes and barns. Some of the buildings are built from stone. Absolutely gorgeous country and here I am traveling at 70 mph with little time to enjoy. The Susquehanna River is crossed in Harrisburg. I debate about stopping early for the night so I can explore some of these farms on the morrow, but it's too cold. I am eager to get into a warmer climate.

I see my first bad accident. A small red sports car is on its roof in the ditch and as traffic inches by directed by police, there's also a black SUV that's rolled over and glass is all over the highway. Not an easy sight to view and my heart pounds as I think how horrible it must be to lose control of a vehicle and hit something at 75 mph.

The interstate passes into Maryland and continues on into West Virginia over the Potomac River where I stop at the visitor center. The woman suggests the Comfort Inn in Martinsburg and I take her offer, grab some brochures on the way out the door, and a short time later, check into the hotel. The odometer reads 13,711.8, which means 277 miles today for a total of 545.7 since leaving home.

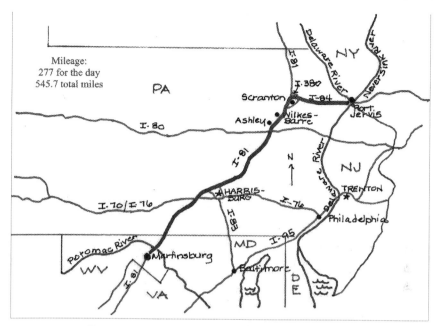

Mileage:
277 for the day
545.7 total miles

From Port Jervis, N.Y. to Martinsburg, W.Va.

A lot of camper trailers with Canadian plates were on the road throughout the day. It seems like most are at this hotel and as I head past the breakfast area, a group of people are chatting in French. I feel I'm in a foreign country and get a vision of families and friends in a camper trailer convoy heading south for the winter and setting up little Canadian communities in Florida. What fun.

This is a much nicer place than the Days Inn from last night and it's cheaper. I'm in Room 203 with a king bed and no stains on the comforter. I settle in and set up the laptop where I check messages and write the blog. Karen's report is similar to last night's; no sign of Freyja, but she's eating and drinking. I wish I would take the time to stop more often and take notes. There are many things I want to mention and can't remember now. However, part of my challenge and adventure is to remember the instances that catch my attention.

By 6 p.m., my brain shuts down. It's time to watch a little TV. Oh, I do miss my DVR where I can fast forward through commercials. Here, I look through the brochures while those annoying ads blare away. I turn the volume down. Commercials are loud, obnoxious and I do not want to bother the neighbors. The two scenic train brochures show neither place is open this time of year. Aww. I crawl into bed around 9:30 p.m.

DAY 3, WEDNESDAY, JANUARY 23

Martinsburg, W. Va. and on to Virginia

Slept better last night, but I'm up at 4 a.m. with another horrible headache. I should have gotten up earlier to take some aspirin. Hopefully, this morning's coffee will be better than yesterday's. It might be the water, too, city water. I can smell it when the tap is turned on. Bottled water is $1.50 out of the machine for a 20 fl. oz. bottle. I bought one last night, probably should've bought two. Yep, should've gone with the bottled water, but at least it's better than yesterday's and I am drinking it. Maybe today I could stop at a store and get a case.

Recollections come up as I journal. There's something about writing in long hand that triggers memory. I want to remember everything that's interesting. The hardest is the highway driving. Yes, it gets one quicker to a destination, but so much is missed along the way. Yet, there are things and vantage points to see from the highway than from another road. For instance, the back of the farms are seen from the interstate and because the route is sometimes higher, much more of the buildings are seen and oftentimes run-down looking; a totally different view than from a front, eye-level view. I like the run-down look.

Writing done, I check over the invoice slid under the door. The rate was $59.50 for the night with a state tax and city/county tax of $3.57 each for a total of $66.64. The breakfast bar has nothing appealing when I go after the luggage trolley. I load up the trolley and haul my things out. During check-out, the lady at the desk tells me of a train station not far away and gives me a map through the city pointing out other interesting sites. She also shows how to get back to the highway without backtracking. She says Martinsburg has some wonderful historical buildings.

It's 9:30 and the skies are sunny with a few clouds. Too bad it has to be so horribly cold, 16 degrees. Gas costs $45.33 at $3.59/gal. I head towards the downtown area.

Martinsburg Roundhouse

Martinsburg is a wonderful city. Some of the buildings are amazing. The train station is down a side street. The road around it is brick. The building is on the side of a steep embankment like it was cut into the hill. The parking area and sidewalks look down on the tracks. Across the tracks are a series of old brick buildings surrounded by a chain link fence. The one on the far left is a long, two-story barracks-like building, then a roundhouse, another building, and ruins of a second roundhouse. An elevated walkway leads from the current station to the historic buildings across the tracks.

I climb the stairs to the main level. Inside are people, who, I guess, are waiting for a train. The Visitor's Center isn't open. I look at the displays then go down a longer flight of stairs in the back to track level. There are a few more people waiting in the entry way avoiding the cold. I go outside and take photographs up and down the tracks. I want to explore the old buildings, but the chain link fencing on the other side of the track prohibits access. It looks like the only way over is via the enclosed walkway from the second story to a tower across the tracks. I want to get over there.

I go back up the flight of stairs to the main floor and over to the stairway leading to the second. A sign says Children's Museum. Will my knees take another flight of stairs? I can't resist a chance to get to those old empty buildings across the tracks which are perhaps the original train station. I gimp my way to the top only to find a closed sign on the door of the overhead walkway. Oh, no, how disappointing. Why couldn't there be a sign at the foot of the stairs? Well, there will be no close inspections of the older part of the station.

Martinsburg Roundhouse

Wait! Is that a whistle? A train is coming! Can I get down these stairs fast enough? I make it outside just in time. Being on a higher level than the tracks, I can see into the open cars as they fly by. Car after car and the contents are black. Is this coal?

I take more pictures and hear another whistle. There's a train coming from the opposite direction. Two trains in one day. How exciting. This one is pulling tanker type cars. There still must be another train due because of the people waiting inside. I debate hanging around.

Brief History Lesson

The railroad reached Martinsburg in 1842 and within the next 7 years, a roundhouse and shops were built. Between May of 1861 and March of 1862, Confederate soldiers under General Stonewall Jackson confiscated, damaged, or destroyed 400 cars and 40 locomotives. Equipment, tools, and a 40 foot roundtable was dismantled and moved to Strasberg and Richmond. Then in Sept.—Oct. 1862, the troops retreating from the Battle of Antietam in Maryland destroyed 38 miles of track and burned the roundhouse and shops.

A new west roundhouse and shops were built by the Baltimore and Ohio Railroad Company in 1866 and the east roundhouse in 1872. One is now only a few walls on the other side of the building to the right of main roundhouse. The main roundhouse is the only completely enclosed cast iron framed roundhouse still standing today. The Great Strike of 1877 began here when workers protested wage reductions. This started the first and biggest strike in this country's history. The Martinsburg Roundhouse Center on 13 acres was in use until the mid-1980s.

Time to Move on

I'm cold. It's time to go on my way. If it was warmer, I'd tour some of the other Civil War era historic places open to the public like the Shenandoah Ballroom. Heading out of town along King Street, the houses are fabulous. I can understand why this street is called King. These are homes that I envision of the old south. The history, architecture, and stone work are quite different from New Hampshire. I am impressed.

The on ramp to I-81S is reached at 10:30. The speed limit is 70 mph. The temperature has risen to 19 degrees and 15 minutes later I cross the Virginia state line and pull in to the first rest stop; 21 degrees, a little further south, a little warmer. I collect brochures and maps. The lady at the visitor center says they don't have scenic trains in Virginia because of insurance. That sounds strange, but such as it is. She does say the Skyline Drive is open and that it continues as the Blue Ridge Parkway. Rte. 66E is only 20 miles away. She specifically says that it only goes east and that it's not part of THE Route 66 that goes west.

A short time later, I take the exit for Rte. 66. There's a decision to make; Skyline Drive or stay on the highway. This cold is so cold. These temperatures are not usual for here, but not unheard of either. The sign for the Skyline Drive points to the next ramp. Do I take it? At the last moment, I turn the wheel and veer off the highway. If I wait until the return trip, it could be snowing and the road closed.

The road narrows and meanders through the city of Front Royal. I stay in the center lane trying to watch for signs in case I need to make a left or right turn. There's traffic on both sides of me and I feel like I'm the only one who doesn't know where she's going. A small sign with a Skyline Drive arrow near a set of lights points left. Geez, they could give a driver a little warning. I just barely squeeze between two vehicles to get into the left lane to make the turn then drive and drive without seeing any other signs. It's nerve wracking and confusing. I'm unsure of the lane and after awhile, I'm not even sure if I am on the right road. The busyness thins and I finally come to the big brown entrance sign.

Skyline Drive

The entrance fee at the little guard shack is $10. It's noon, the odometer reads 13,766.2, and it is 21 degrees. The park ranger with his southern drawl tells me that if I want to do any hiking, I'll be alone on the trails. That won't be a problem. In this cold it's highly unlikely any hiking will happen. He says it would be better for photographs if the sun wasn't shining. I'll take what I can get.

The road narrows and winds up the mountain and as I drive along, I think, what sun? It's quite cloudy. Trees and landscape on both sides of the road are brown, gray and colorless with dried yellow grasses. This is just like late winter back home after the snow melts. This isn't such a big deal. A flash of bright blue against the dull colors catches my eye as a flock of bluebirds flies from the ground to the trees. Poor little things, bet they didn't expect it to be this cold.

The first stop is at Shenandoah Valley Overlook, elevation 1,390 ft. I jump out and run around to the passenger side to don sweater and coat. The temperature is 20 degrees, but with the wind it's much colder. I grab the camera and hurry to the edge of the drop off. Wow, what a breathtaking scene! The vista opens up in a humongous arc with the land dropping down and across the valley to other mountains far away. Even with some blue in the sky, the valley is a bit colorless and the distant mountains are in a blue fog. Still, the view is absolutely spectacular. It's amazing how far I can see. Photographs are not going to do this justice. A pileated woodpecker on a tree flies off as I move closer.

Back off come coat and sweater and I scoot around to the driver's side. Brrr. After going around one corner, there is a whole row of bushes that still has green leaves. That's surprising. I wonder what they are. The view ahead opens up as the road curves to the left. Over the top of the rock wall along the right side there is nothing but sky. If I drove straight, I'd be airborne. The road continues to twist and climb.

The next stop is at the Dickey Ridge Visitor Center. The temperature is 19 degrees. The building is closed. I get out and go through the same routine of donning sweater and coat to take scenery photos. There is a picnic area and trails. On a nice day, it would be great to explore. I walk out to the edge where a bench is placed for relaxing. How many times could I say amazing, breath-taking, fabulous? I wish it was warmer.

A Seat on the Edge

Coat and sweater come back off so I can drive on. The road continues to climb up and winds around one way then the other. First overlooks are off to the right then a couple to the left and it alternates. I stop at every pull off, every overlook. It's cold, brutally cold with the wind. The temperatures drop the higher the elevation. After another stop for photos, I keep my coat and sweater on which means I don't do up the seat belt. It's a nuisance as there are so many stops. A lot of photos are taken even though the vistas lack color. The rocks, trees, and grasses are fascinating even though they, too, lack brilliant color. Water is a frozen tumble over rocks. Signal Knob Overlook is almost a 180-degree panoramic vista with the Shenandoah River a teensy weensy meandering line far, far below.

The road still continues up and around; Goony Run Overlook; Compton Overlook, elevation 2,400 ft. with the temperature at 16 degrees; Jenkins Gap and still the road winds round with long curves and magnificent vistas. I pull over at Hogwallow Overlook with elevation of 2,665 ft.; Browntown Valley at 2,890 ft. and Little Devil's Stairs at 3,120 feet. By this point, I'm tired of it. The views are similar huge open vistas that are dimmed by the bluish mountains in the far distance. (There's a reason why they are called the Blue Ridge Mountains.)

The road runs down, then back up to the highest point at Hogback Overlook, elevation 3,385 ft. I stop for one last time. It is 13 degrees. Photos of the more than 180-degree view are taken, but I'm ready for this to end. If it was later in the year with more color and warmer temperatures to allow walking the trails, this would be more stunning and enjoyable.

Finally, it's down, down, down and it feels like I am never going to find my way back to civilization. Eventually the Thornton Gap Entrance Station gate is reached at the intersection of Rte. 211. It's 2 p.m. with the odometer reading 13,797.4 and temperature at 18 degrees.

I pull off the road to check the map. The road continues as the Blue Ridge Parkway into North Carolina. Original plans had me going that route to visit a Vanderbilt mansion in Asheville, but I can't take any more of these similar views and dreary colors. Although I have some disappointment in the lack of color and clarity, I am glad I did this. If I hadn't, I would have regretted it. Even with the colorless vistas, it's still a wonder to see. It must be totally amazing in the summertime. Rte. 211 heads towards Washington, DC. I'll be able to pick up Rte. 17S before the big city.

Leaving the Skyline

The road off the ridge is a trip! It goes down, way down with steep hairpin curves, some at 90 degrees. I almost have to come to a stop to make it around those corners. As I gingerly make my way down the mountainside, I am reminded me of a sign I saw at the beginning, High Motorcycle Fatalities Next 3 Miles. Oh, my, gosh, I can see why on this road! It's kind of fun, kind of scary, and 100 percent attention has to be paid at all times. It twists and turns, first to the left, then to the right with trees on steep banks so high on one side that the tops can't be seen. The other side is a steep ravine with a brook far below. This would be a terrible road to be on during even simple rain showers . . . or at night, for that matter. Going off the pavement would certainly mean death.

The road finally levels out in Sperryville. I like this area. It feels like the middle of nowhere, relaxing and quiet. I'm tempted to stop for a couple of photos of dilapidated buildings, but it's getting late and I haven't eaten. Rte. 211 is an enjoyable, peaceful drive with two lanes eastbound, a wide grassy median and two lanes westbound. Periodically, there would be a U-turn or side road access. The speed limit is 55, traffic is light and further along, I do pull over long enough to take a couple photos out the window of the farm land. More green trees, pine and possibly yew or spruce line the road and that reminds me, I saw very few evergreens along Skyline Drive.

Rte. 17S is picked up in Warrenton, a city where the traffic is again heavy and signs small and far and few between. Again I wonder if I'm still on the right road. In spite of keeping an eye on the traffic, I get glimpses of beautiful houses and farms. A few are made with colored stone making the buildings look like irregular patchwork quilts. I really like these.

Settling in for the Night

I am more than ready to stop for the night by the time Fredericksburg is reached, about 4 p.m. I pull over to get out the coupon booklet on places to stay. Although I'd been thinking about a steak, I am too tired. I choose a Comfort Inn Suites with an indoor pool. The odometer reads 13,865.8. I only drove 154 miles for the day, a total of 699.7 from home.

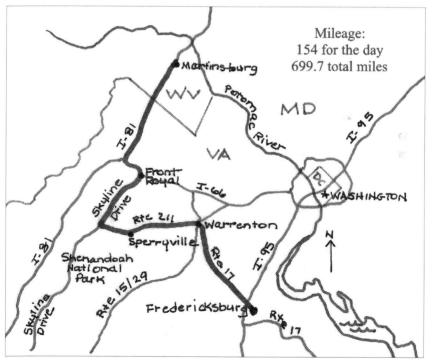

From Martinsburg, W.Va. to Fredericksburg, Va. via the SkyLine Drive

I comment on the cold weather and the two women behind the desk look at each and laugh.

"It's not usually this cold, but not unusual, either," says one.

"At least it kills all the ticks and fleas," adds the other.

I walk away wondering if fleas and ticks are a problem in the hotels down here and tell myself it can't be. They must be talking about outside. Then again, a lot of the hotels are pet friendly. No, no, no, don't even go there! I have to believe these hotels are clean.

Lasagna is being served at 6:30, but as I haven't eaten anything all day, I can't wait. I settle in to Room 102, last down on the first floor and order pizza. I set up the laptop and turn it on. Then I notice there are internet plugs. Perhaps I don't need to be using my surge protector. I unplug the laptop and plug it into the hotel's outlet. I hit a button on the computer and the screen goes dark blue.

No, no, no, what did I do? One of my biggest fears on this trip is to lose internet access. I unplug it and plug it back in; still a dark blue screen. I hit every button on the keyboard . . . nothing. I am panicking. What am I going to do?

I dig out the cell phone and call Annette, owner and publisher of the *InterTown Record*, the local paper for which I work. The phone immediately goes black though it's ringing. Annette's voice mail picks up. I try to hang up. Nothing works. I push every button. The phone is still dark. It must have shut off. I go back to punching keys on the laptop trying to get something to happen. Suddenly the phone starts talking about time being taken up on the voice mail. Oh, no, the phone wasn't shut off after all. It was still connected to Annette's phone. I open the back of the phone and pull out the battery.

The pizza arrives, but I'm too distracted and frantic to eat. I don't know what to do. I put the battery back in the cell phone and it turns on. I make a few calls before I am able to get someone to help. With each call, the phone turns black the moment it starts ringing and none of the buttons work. After each call, I have to pull out the battery to turn off the phone. I get hold of my daughter-in-law, Sophia, and she is able to help me get the laptop up and running. Of course, it was something easy – I didn't hold the button down long enough to get it to turn back on. She has no idea what's wrong with the phone.

By this time, it's almost 6 p.m. Guess I could have done the lasagna dinner. I gobble down a couple slices of cold pizza while checking messages. There's one from Karen. My heart drops at her words. When she went over to the house, all the registers were cold. She called the oil company and arranged for a serviceman. When he arrived, he found the boiler out. He cleaned out the sludge and got it fired up. In the meantime, the pipes froze. When Karen turned on faucets in the upstairs sink, the water would not run nor did the tank in the toilet fill when flushed. Water was running earlier, so the pipes hadn't been frozen long. With the thermostats turned up the water should thaw with no problems.

I message her back. Do I need to come home? This will be heartbreaking to cut the trip short. She assures me that everything is under control. She will give me an update tomorrow. With the heat working, she's probably right. I am so grateful that she feels I don't need to come home. I can't thank her enough.

After writing my blog, I decide to check out the pool. It's beside the dining area and as they are serving that lasagna dinner, I certainly don't want to be parading by people in a swim suit. I walk down about 7:20. There isn't anyone around, so I return to the room and put on my suit. I have the pool all to myself. It's a little chilly, but it feels so good. I love to swim and never do. I only spend about 20 minutes, but the entire time I am moving and not touching bottom if I can help it. It's cold when I get out. I quickly towel off with a hotel towel, wrap my own big towel from home around me to absorb excess water, throw my wrap over that and head back to the room hoping to not drip down the hallway. I'm not a person to lie around a pool area.

The heater in this room is very noisy. I watch a little television. Ugh, I hate commercials and after a couple shows, call it a night.

DAY 4, THURSDAY, JANUARY 24

I Want Out of Virginia

I'm up early as usual having slept well in spite of the noisy heater coming on every few minutes. It drives me crazy. Foremost on my mind is the need to find a Verizon Store to get the cell phone issue resolved. I check messages and write in the journal. I'm re-thinking the journal writing now that I'm putting all the information in the blog. On the one hand, it's doing things twice. On the other, thoughts often surface while I'm writing in longhand. At this point, the journal should only contain what doesn't get put in the blog. I want to be able to get on the road as early as possible.

The invoice slipped under the door show the night's charges are $65 for the room, $3.25 for state tax and $3.25 for occupancy for a total of $71.50. I want to import photos taken yesterday, but it's getting late and I want to look over maps.

After showering and getting dressed, I head to the breakfast area. A lady shows me how to use the waffle maker. It's on a timer. Eww, it's gooey on the inside. I eat a couple pieces of bacon and drink a small cup of orange juice. That's all my stomach will take. I chat with a nice woman from Ocala, Fla. She says something about last night's snow. Oh, I didn't know, hadn't looked out a window. She also tells me that Savannah is a wonderful place to visit and that they have trolley tours.

The woman at the desk tells me there's a huge Verizon Store at the next exit off I-95S. These people are so nice. One of the guys brushes the snow off my truck. I leave the Comfort Suites Inn about 10 a.m. The temperature is 27 degrees. I only burned about half a tank of gas yesterday, so can put off filling up. A short time later I'm looking for the Verizon Store amidst watching out for vehicles in the three lanes of traffic. Good thing I stop for a light. I glance to the left and there's the store in a little strip mall. I don't know what that woman was thinking saying it's huge.

An hour is spent inside as the young man plays around with my phone. Finally he says I either have to buy a new phone or send this one back to the manufacturer (Samsung.) Buy a new phone? This one's only about a month old. I'm not buying a new phone! It's only been used it three times. I am not happy and as I get back on I-95S with a 70 mph speed limit, my thoughts are racing with this phone issue. I am so disgusted and discouraged. I just want to get away from here. At this point, I no longer care about Williamsburg. I just want to get to warmer weather. I want out of Virginia.

I have to calm down. It doesn't do me any good to get angry. I practice breathing exercises (one with my eyes open.) This is a boring section of driving anyway. No scenery. I do have to pay attention to traffic. It's hard to get me out of this funk when there's nothing interesting to grab my attention. After awhile I realize that there are more pine trees than I've been seeing; spots of dark green against the dull yellow-browns of the winter season.

Coming into Richmond, I-95 goes straight while Rte. 295 loops out around the city and would be the way to Williamsburg. I have to make a choice. Going straight through the city might be quicker, but there will be more traffic and scarier. I opt for the long way around which turns out to be a long, boring drive. The one highlight is crossing the James River on the 4,680 foot-long Varina-Enon Bridge. It has a vertical navigational clearance of 150 feet. The road surface is cement with cement K rails. At the apex are tall pillars with bridge struts (cable stayed) holding them together. Oh, what I wouldn't give to be able to take a picture, but there is no stopping.

I'm hungry. I want to get back on I-95 before finding a place to stop. My face feels flushed and I hope I'm not going to be sick. It's probably just lack of food. I am in Emporia when I see a sign for a Cracker Barrel. I've been craving a steak and by 1 p.m., I'm seated at a table where I order a 10 oz. rib-eye. I can't wait. The waitress brings the dish and I immediately send back the baked potato. It was so cold the butter wouldn't even start melting. I cut up the steak. I swear of the 10 oz., five was fat. From watching the cooking shows, I know that meat has to have fat for flavor and tenderness, but half the meal is an inedible hunk of fat. It's ridiculous to pay for that. There's a reason I seldom eat steak.

Still, the meal is filling and even though I can't eat it all, I order blackberry cobbler for dessert. I feel the need for some sugar. I only eat half of that. With a full stomach, I feel much better and I'm ready to get back on the road. I get gas at Exxon for $3.53/gal. My plan is to get into North Carolina and find a place for the night. I cross the state line at 2:18 p.m. It has warmed up to a whopping 34 degrees. At the visitor center, I pick up a few brochures and the woman shows me hotel coupons. She says she "can't really suggest a hotel," but she "kind of leans towards the Quality Inn." Out in the truck, I look further at the coupon book. Something bothers me about the Quality Inn. I don't know what, but I decide to listen to my intuition. I like the Comfort Suites and there's one at exit 143. I'll shoot for that.

Back on the interstate, I notice more green on the sides of the roads and beyond. Bushes, more pines, and even a hint of green in the grass. I miss the exit for the Comfort Suites and end up on Rte. 64E, another major highway. East is towards Cape Hatteras. I decide not to turn around. I'm on an adventure. Guess my plan for stopping early isn't going to pan out. Maybe I'm meant to go this way.

This turns out to be a long drive. Am I ever going to get to the coast? Should I have gone back to I-95? I don't dare look at the map while I'm driving. I feel I've been driving forever and it's time to stop and at the next exit that advertises a Comfort Inn, I turn off the highway, take a left at the end of the ramp and on and on. Where the hell am I?

The inn is in Tarboro. No indoor pool. Aww, I was spoiled last night. The odometer reads 14072.9, 207.1 miles since yesterday, a total of 906.8 since leaving home. What's great about this place is that it's not near the highway so I won't have to listen to that noise tonight. The hotel is pretty inside and the lady puts me at the end near the front desk. She says that they always put single women close. My room number is 102 like last night except I was the last room down.

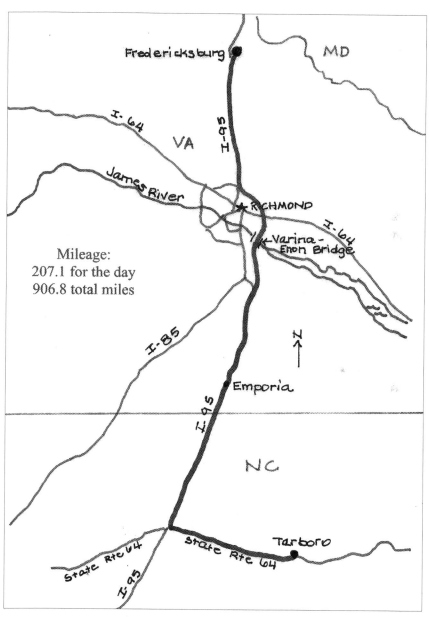

Mileage:
207.1 for the day
906.8 total miles

From Fredericksburg, Va. To Tarboro, N.C.

I like this room. It doesn't feel crowded. I'm settled in by 4:30 and call Don to let him know I'm in safe for the night. No answer. I check messages and write the blog. I look at my work schedule as it is Thursday and by 7 p.m., I am working on my weekly column. One of the LTEs (letters to the editor) for the week also has information that will work in the column so I tighten that up. That's done unless I add some personal comments in the beginning. I usually add bits about the weather or critters in the backyard. This time will be about my trip to let the readers know about my travels and kind of bring them along.

I next work on the community calendar, but by 8 p.m., I'm winding down. There's still more to do and more LTEs. One thing about writing in Microsoft Word where there are auto corrects, I forget how much speech differs from formal writing. I try to leave out the first word (especially saying "I," "There's," or "It's" so often) and the fragment message comes up. If I write, "Went to Concord yesterday," which sounds perfectly okay in my head, it comes up as fragment until I write "I went to Concord." I like the auto review though, because it helps me be a better writer and I do eventually want to put my journey into a book. And when I write, I don't want to have someone else do a lot of editing. I'd rather do it right the first time. Writing is not exactly like speaking even with the words "talking" in my head.

Annette sends a message saying I should call Verizon and insist they help me or give me a new phone. She's right, but the thought of spending an hour on the phone with them is not appealing. I have things to do, places to go, and sights to see. Dealing with these types of issues is upsetting. It's just not something I'm good at. I get frustrated, angry, break down in tears; not very adult or professional. At almost sixty years old, my emotions should be better under control. It's funny, but in some aspects and in spite of all my training, I am more emotional now than I've been in many years. I like to think that's a good thing.

After an hour and a half of TV watching re-runs of "Chopped," I crawl into bed.

DAY 5, FRIDAY, JANUARY 25

Bridges and Moss-Covered Trees

Happy day! I'm in the middle of nowhere North Carolina, not even halfway between Interstate 95 and Hatteras. That steak dinner I had yesterday, the first heavy solid food I've had in awhile, hit with a vengeance about midnight. Not a big deal. At least I'm not feeling sick or anything like that. Hopefully it will all work out of me before I leave. It didn't help that noisy people were slamming doors and yakking half the night.

I've now stayed in four hotels and none have standard pillows. The pillows are half pillows and there are usually four to six on a bed. I like them. A head doesn't take up a great big pillow anyway. These smaller ones also work great as a back support when sitting in the chairs or on couches. I look over brochures and maps. Do I go back to I-95 or continue on to Rte. 17S? I'm leaning towards the latter. I don't want to backtrack. I don't know if I can make Charleston today. I'll need to stop early to work. Friday is often my main work day along with Saturday mornings. The hotel invoice shows the room charge $72 and the state tax, $4.86.

It's after 7:30 a.m. I am dressed and ready for the day. Perhaps if I go down to the breakfast area, I might get conversation and ideas on things to see around here. I really didn't do any sightseeing yesterday. There's a train track nearby. Could there possibly be an old depot? Ugh, the thought of eating anything right now isn't appealing.

I leave the Comfort Inn at 9:45 a.m. The skies are overcast and it's 28 degrees. The lady at the desk suggested going back to I-95, but I don't want to go west. I get on Rte. 64 heading east and very happy with my choice. The highway, though still divided, is quiet this time of day. There is little traffic. Every so often are the crossroads for access to side streets and U-turns. The countryside is farmland. I like it – until I pass something that is shocking – a black and tan puppy dead in the middle of the road. How horrible. There aren't any houses nearby and all I can speculate is he jumped out of someone's pickup truck. And they didn't even stop! I hate seeing things like that. It's upsetting.

I'm trying to stop thinking about that puppy when a large pond is passed. What's that white bird flying? Are those swans in that pond? There are a lot of them. Can it be? I've never seen so many swans in one place. With no traffic, I can stop, but by the time I slow down and pull over, I have passed the first pond and come to a stop beside another with more of those white birds on the far side. They look like swans, but I didn't know swans could fly. Many have disappeared by the time I grab the camera and extend the lens. They still look like swans. I take pictures the best I can out the window. I'm excited. There has to be about fifty of them.

I continue on my way and come to Rte. 17S sooner than expected. There is more green grass and green fields. How nice after all the dull colors of winter. My head is on a swivel looking first to the left, then to the right. This is a more leisurely drive even at 55 mph. The temperature rises to 34 degrees. The highway narrows to a regular two-lane road and the sides are dotted with white. I remember seeing this yesterday and thought it was snow, but here it doesn't seem right. The fields are white dotted, too. Could it be cotton? I pull over and pick some off the ground. It IS cotton! Wow, it must blow off the plants like a thick, heavy milkweed or dandelion puffs and it's almost like the cotton balls bought at the store except it's denser and dirty from being on the ground.

I keep it and also pick up a couple of pine cones. I take a couple photos of a nearby dilapidated building. A lot of run-down buildings are along this route. There are also some high-flying birds which look like vultures. When I look back to the road, a bunch of them are on the ground up ahead and as I drive by, I see they are feeding on a dead deer. Oh, I cannot resist, I have to turn around. Of course, they fly off when I stop. These are not our turkey vultures. These are bigger with more brown on them and their wings are beautiful. Hopefully, I got some good photos of them in flight.

I drive out into a field to take pictures of an abandoned building in which the trees have grown up so close around it that it looks like the derelict is imprisoned.

The roofs of the homes along this route are flatter than those seen in the northeast. Most of these buildings are run down and in need of paint jobs. Many are modular or mobile homes. After awhile it dawns on me that these are one-story houses. I wonder if these are the homes of farm hands. I also notice quite a few small houses have the name of a church or chapel. Maybe this is so people don't have to go far to worship.

The road eventually widens with a big area between north and south bound lanes. Crossing the Tar River is a trip! This is an Oh-My-Gosh bridge; high above swamp and river where the Tar River becomes the Pamlico. I see my first moss-laden trees. They look like huge gray ghosts creeping out of the swamps. Are these cypresses? The moss on some trees looks like furry gray creatures hanging from limbs and wrapped around trunks. The highway climbs. The entire bridge is cement with K-rail sides and it goes up and up. Aaargh, to be able to get photos! The river is sleepy and I want to look and look. There's not even a break-down lane, not that I'd dare stop on a bridge in this traffic. But I oh, so want to! My mind is babbling.

These first sights of the moss-covered trees have me practically jumping in the seat. Soon I approach another bridge. This one crosses the Neuse River into New Bern. I don't even know how to describe it and if I wanted a picture of that other bridge, this one is the most impressive I've ever seen. The cement roadway makes the tires give off a funny whistle and it's like driving up a hill. Two lanes between cement walls going up and up make me feel a little claustrophobic and above there is nothing but sky. This would be tough for anyone afraid of heights.

And the VIEW! If I thought that other bridge was Oh, My God, this one is OHHH-MY-GODDD! It's scary high especially with traffic moving at 60 mph. This bridge immediately turns into another bridge crossing the Trent River from which there is an off ramp which is also a bridge and clover leafs. How anything like this could be built is totally amazing. I have GOT to come home this way. Maybe I'll figure out where to get photos. Then to top it off, the bridge continues on through swampland with more of those moss-covered trees. These tall, colorless giants, naked except for the furry moss hanging in long clumps, trees that seem to come out of the wetlands like zombies creeping up to grab travelers have me squealing inside with excitement. The bridge eventually gives way to "normal" dry land, but my mind continues to run wild.

I take the Rte. 17S By-pass around New Bern, a long, desolate stretch with pines on both sides of the road not allowing any view. At this point, I don't know that my mind could take any more. I stop in Jacksonville, N.C. at Applebees for lunch at 12:30. Odometer reads 14,199.1; it's 37 degrees with a light rain. The waitress tells me that it is two and a half hours to South Carolina. Applebees has televisions everywhere. The Weather Channel predicts 50 degrees for tomorrow. I'll believe that when I see it.

I'm tired after the meal and decide not to push for South Carolina today. The gas tank is filled at a Hess station in Hampstead paying $3.37/gal. A little bit later, I pass through Jacksonville, home of the Marine Corps Base Camp Lejeune. In Wilmington, I pass the entrance for the USS North Carolina Battleship Memorial. It is huge. I can see it from the highway. That would be cool to visit. I've never been on a big battleship, but it's cold, I'm tired, it's getting late and I need to find a hotel. This is another reason to come home this way. Hopefully, it'll be warmer.

I check into Room 211 in a Comfort Suites in Leland at 3 p.m. The odometer reads 14,268, a drive of 195.1 miles today for a total of 1,101.9 I make use of both the indoor swimming pool and laundry facilities.

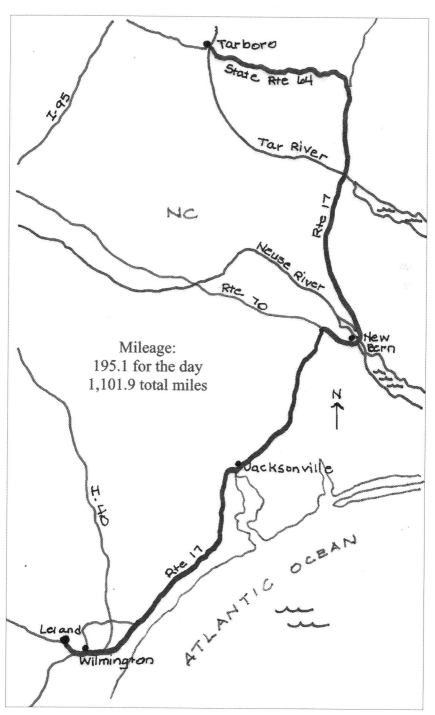

Mileage:
195.1 for the day
1,101.9 total miles

From Tarboro, N.C. to Leland, N.C.

I check back home. Karen reports the water is running in the faucets. She is a God-send; not only for taking care of my precious kitty, but for handling the unforeseen issues. I'm so glad I don't have to abort this trip. I write the blog and finish the community calendar. I'll do the LTEs tomorrow.

I import the photos taken so far onto the laptop. Oh, crap, RAW images don't show up until after I change them to jpegs. What a nuisance to not be able to view the photo first. It's time consuming to open the icon only to find it's not a photo I want to use right away. I do edit a couple and load them on to Facebook. I get out the manual to read how to delete photos from the memory card. (I am able to do this from the pc when I work at home.) I also change the camera setting to RAW and Jpeg instead of RAW only.

By this time, I'm ready to relax and maybe watch a little TV. I heat the leftover Crispy Orange Chicken from Applebees in the microwave. As usual, I crawl into bed about 9:30. Will I reach Charleston tomorrow?

DAY 6, SATURDAY, JANUARY 26

Heading to Charleston

The cushion of this chair I sit in, that fake leather stuff, squishes when I sit and makes the sound like squeaking air out of a balloon. Pshhhewwww. Or like those old war movies and the sound with bombs whistling when dropping and before they explode. Maybe I should be thankful I don't have an exploding chair, ha ha.

The price for this room was quoted at $89 for the night. This morning I get the bill and there's a state tax of $6.01, a city/county tax of $2.67, and an occupancy tax of $.89. As I keep saying, I'd rather be given the total price up front. I don't like surprises. Reminds me of the time I rented a car in Arizona for a hundred something for the week and when I returned, I was shocked to find I had to pay almost $300 because of taxes, insurance add-ons and other fees.

I study the map of South Carolina. The state line should be reached in an hour from leaving here. I do a few LTEs and check the web for Boone Plantation as I'm hoping to go there today. Drat, it's closed until February 3. This is another reason to come back this way on my return trip. However, there are plenty of others to visit. Brookgreen Gardens in Murrells Inlet which is just south of Myrtle Beach is first on the list. Next would be Hampton Plantation, then I'll head on down to Charleston where Cypress Gardens, Magnolia Plantation, Fort Sumter, and Charleston itself will keep me occupied. I'm excited about visiting plantations, learning more history, and seeing these properties in person.

Researching online, it looks like some of those places may take all day. There will be lots of walking and possible train and boat rides. Imagine boating through cypress swamps! Perhaps Charleston will be a three-day lay-over. It'll be good to have a home base for a bit and not to have to pack up every day. I'm sure when I stop at the visitor center upon crossing the state border I will find even more things to do. At least the temperatures are supposed to be warmer.

I pack up for the day and leave the hotel at 10:10 a.m. under pale blue skies with a faint overcast. It's 41 degrees. It rained during the night, but my vehicle is still the dirtiest around. I get on Rte. 17S and less than an hour later, I cross the state line into South Carolina and pull into the visitors center. The temperature has risen six degrees. Yea!

There are no other tourists, so all three ladies behind the desk chat with me. We discuss hotels and I decide on the Holiday Inn Riverview in Charleston and the reservation is made. It offers free shuttle service to the downtown area. That will be easier and less scary if I don't have to drive into the city, plus it costs to park. What I find interesting is that as friendly and as helpful as anyone could want, people are very tight lipped about the neighboring state. I ask a question and the answer is, "Hmmm, yes, well, we can't really comment on that." I leave with a bunch of brochures on places to visit.

Back on Rte. 17S, the drive is again a tedious, 55-60 mph and uneventful. Myrtle Beach is stop-and-go with 45-55 mph between lights and this is the straight through, not Ocean Boulevard. The welcome lady had said that would be even slower. This is a shopping mecca; miles and miles of stores, shops, and places to eat. It's overwhelming with south and northbound three lanes wide. I mostly stay in the middle. The senses are assailed with sign after sign, some too small to read until right up close. By then, if I'd wanted to stop, I would be going by. With the traffic, I don't dare look around much. Hurry to the next light, stop then hurry to the next. I don't like this at all! It feels like it takes forever to get through this section.

Past Myrtle Beach, I begin watching for signs for Murrells Inlet where I will make my first stop at Brookgreen Gardens which was highly recommended by Bob and Jane. Ah, there's a sign for Murrells Inlet and I zip into the left lane and turn before realizing I did not see a sign for Brookgreen Gardens. This ends up being a loop through a residential area and back out onto Rte. 17. A short time later, I do see the sign I am looking for and it is a right hand turn.

Brookgreen Gardens, Murrells Inlet, S.C.

Brookgreen Gardens is an amazing place to visit, one of the top public gardens in the country, and my first to a southern plantation area. It cost $14 to just get in to the gardens. With all there is to see and do, I can see why the ticket is good for seven days. There's 9,100 acres which includes an outdoor museum, many gardens, trails, sculptures, zoo, wildlife, boat dock and more. The Butterfly House isn't open until April and there are no boat rides this time of year.

The property was once the Oaks Plantation and the original house and slave village is an archeological site at a remote location. Its walking trails are accessible by a Brookgreen vehicle. Today I am only going to explore the gardens and other areas are put on my agenda to visit at a future date. I put the map and brochure in my pocket. I like to explore on my own without being influenced. Plus, I find it awkward to manipulate maps, camera, and walking stick.

Arched Entrance

From the entrance, a covered walkway leads to the gift shop. I don't want to consider buying anything I will have to carry as I walk. There are choices. Right, left, or straight. I go straight and pass through a sculpture pavilion. I'm not interested in sculptures, though they are amazing from the few I see in the hallway. I am here for the gardens. I pass through that building and come out into a beautiful courtyard. The restaurant nearby is closed for renovations. Guess I won't be having lunch here. I continue strolling along garden paths. Sculptures are everywhere, often the focal point in these gardens.

There are specific designs and paths leading from one garden to another. Some are like mazes with paths in and around. Each garden is separated by a wall of taller bushes and/or trees with entranceways between them. I ooh and aah to myself over the green plants and small trees. Some are too sculpted with the neatly trimmed hedges almost mathematically precise. Still, I like it. How nice it is, after the dull colors of winter, to see pansies, daffodils, and narcissus in bloom.

I am thankful for my walking stick. It may be a bit of a hassle when I'm trying to balance it to use two hands on the camera when taking pictures, but it makes a difference in where and how far I can walk. It's especially helpful when doing stairs or inclines. I don't know the names of the plants and I wish for a guide, but I am alone except for a couple other visitors who are far and few between. Sometimes I feel like I am the only one here.

I wander from garden to garden each with its own unique traits. What most impress me are the H-U-G-E trees sporting that moss. Now that I see them up close, they are even more massive. I'm not sure three or four men putting their arms around these giants could touch fingers. The lady at the welcome center had been hesitant when asked about the trees on which the moss grows. She gave me the answer of oaks, but the trees in these gardens do not have leaves like the oaks in New England. These trees have kind of a rhododendron-look leaf. I look for little info signs, but for the longest time, the only ones explain about the sculptures. After finally seeing a couple small signs, I decide these must be magnolias.

Do magnolias grow that big and have such enormous trunks? Some of the limbs are as wide as I or wider! Some are held up with cable and many have long strands of moss dripping from them. Yes, it reminds me of water that has frozen while dripping from rocks, like stalactites, like the tattered rags hanging off zombies.

Another familiar, but not quite the same, plant has red, yellow, or pink hibiscus-type flowers, but the leaves again look like the rhododendron family. I see a sign that says camellia. Most of these flowers are just about gone by with many blossoms already dropped to the ground. Even the fallen-turning-brown blossoms have a beauty to them.

There are other buildings holding various sculpture displays, but I stay outside on the paths. I come across a blonde, bark less, leafless tree with that moss on it. This is weird! It looks naked. A little sign identifies it as a crepe myrtle. I continue to follow paths passing from one garden to another until I pass through an opening and leave the manicured gardens for a wooded area.

I follow a dirt road down the hill to the river. There's a labyrinth. On a bench, I take time to write a poem.

Beyond the Labyrinth

Beyond the Labyrinth
lies a river of coffee colored water
whose cream has set too long
its muddy surface
reflecting dried yellow saw grass

Gray ghost skeletons
creep from the swamps
their raggedy moss-tattered garments
drip from crooked limbs
in a haunted scene from months' past

After days of freezing cold
it's nice to feel the sun's warmth
silent, meditative, restful
like this lazy river

Cardinal red adds bright spots
against brown leaves and dead grass
wind whispers through saw grass
breathe in . . . breathe out . . .
Listen . . . liii..stennnn . . .

The labyrinth winds in and around
my soul follows its path
follows the curving river
finds its way back

After days of freezing cold
it's nice to feel the sun's warmth.

I follow a grassy path along the river on a raised section of land. This looks to be some kind of a dike between the river and a pond.

Brief History Lesson

This section was part of an earthen dike built around the rice field. A rice trunk, a long wooden structure, usually a hollowed out cypress log, was built into the dike with a flood gate on either end to regulate water flow between the tidal river on the right and the rice field on the left.

There are palm trees, too, more than one variety, and lots of saw palmetto which is the State Tree of South Carolina. Those leaves remind me of many fingered hands. I love this! These gardens are wonderful and all the different plants are amazing. I occasionally pass other people, but for the most part, my meandering is solitary. Just the way I like it.

There is much more to see and many paths to further travel, but it's getting late. I want to make Charleston by 4 p.m. My body is beginning to ache and I can't walk much further. I've not eaten since having a banana at 9 a.m. This is the most walking I've done in a very long time. I make my way back to the gift shop and pick up a few postcards. Maybe someday I can come back.

Charleston

The welcome lady also told me that there isn't anything past Georgetown. She was right, but I eventually come to an entire section called Sweet Grass Alley. This consists of miles of periodic side-of-the-road skeletal set ups, some holding baskets and other things made with sweet grass. I get the impression that many of the sellers have laid claim to certain booths as I see signs like Kathy's Sweet Grass Baskets. I'm tempted to stop, but don't. Then I pass a section where new sidewalks have been installed. I feel bad for the vendors along this strip. With a speed limit of 55-60, there isn't any place for customers to safely park.

To get into Charleston, Rte. 17 crosses the Wando and Cooper Rivers. Oh, my, here we go again. I feel like screaming (with excitement) going over these bridges. Is this called a single bridge with cloverleaves or is it considered multiple bridges? The road narrows, its surface concrete with cement railings on both sides and the vehicle tires take on a higher toned whine and thump, thump, thump as each section is traversed. It goes up, up, and over and then goes up even higher and over. Aieeeee!!! But look at the VIEWS. Wait, I can't look at the views, too much traffic and turns – bridges that curve and have off ramps and on ramps and have other bridges and roadways that cross over and under. Aaargghh, freaky!

Talk about heart pounding and feeling intimidated and scared. Hey, I'm a country gal. I don't even like driving through Manchester, N.H., and I would never go to Boston, yet here I am in a far away state and taking on situations that scare the daylights out of me. No wonder I'm thinking of holing up for a few days to rest.

Coming down from the bridge, my brain is about fried. Interstates 95 and 93 in New Hampshire are nothing like these roads. The highway narrows between the tall buildings and it's stop and go through the middle of the city with three lanes running north and south, traffic turning right and left at traffic lights, and ramps and vehicles passing on both sides. I stay in the middle lane as I don't know if I'll be making a left or right. The south and northbound lanes split again before the bridge over the Ashley River. The hotel sits on land across the river between the south and northbound lanes. It's unmistakable as it rises high above everything else in the area. I'm not seeing any sign where to turn.

Is that my turn; a left dirt section beside the hotel? It's hard to tell with construction along the highway. I see a sign that says, No Left Turn then I'm by the hotel. Drat, drat, drat! What do I do now? I have to go further south and find a way to turn around. The next set of lights is also No Left Turn and I go down further. I pull into a left turn lane to find it has no set of lights. At 4 o'clock on a Saturday afternoon, traffic is not forgiving and there are three lanes to cross. I can't get back into the travel lanes to go down to the next set of lights. I have to be patient. Finally, there's a break in the traffic and I scoot across. I take that road a short distance to turn around. I make my way back to Rte. 17, this time heading north.

The hotel comes up again on the left and just before that, two routes, one from the right and one from the left merge onto Rte. 17 creating more traffic at the crucial point where I need to get into the hotel lane. I cut across two lanes of traffic earning a blaring horn. Yikes. My heart is pounding as I pull in the parking lot and circle around to find a space to park.

Whew, I'm here. I'm safe. The odometer is at 14,436.2. I've driven 168.2 miles today and 1,270.1 since home.

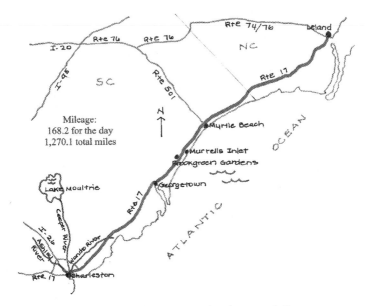

From Leland, N.C. to Charleston, S.C.

This inn is a round building with 15 stories.

Holiday Inn Riverview

The top is called the Harbor View Restaurant. Oh, it hurts getting out of the truck. I need the walking stick. Maybe I did too much today. I hobble my way up the steps into the lobby. I tell him that I want to stay at least two nights. It'll feel good to not mess around with luggage for a day or drive as there is free shuttle service to downtown. I go for the more expensive water view and he says that the price is normally $120 per night, but I can have it for $89. (It'll probably be over $100 with all the taxes.) I'm given the choice of floor three, five, or eleven. I choose the middle and immediately regret it. Why didn't I take the higher? It's me, playing it safe, always taking the middle road.

I sign in, grab a trolley from around the corner and head out to the truck. One of my suitcases is open and I dump all my undies and bras on the pavement. People ignore me. I stuff things inside feeling embarrassed. It's not easy dragging the trolley up the ramp while using my walking stick. The elevators are in the center of the building. I push the button for the fifth floor noting that there is none for 13 and after 14, the next button says Restaurant. Do you call that the 15th floor even though there's no 13?

I take a right out of the elevator. I didn't realize what it would be like in a round building. It feels strange not having any straight corridors. There's almost a dizzying effect. Doors for rooms 512 and 514 are kind of squished together; a narrow entranceway to access the two rooms. I put my key card in the slot for 512 and struggle to push the heavy door open and hold it open while pulling the luggage cart inside bumping against the door.

I turn around. Ah, round building means the rooms are pie shaped with the narrow end to the door, the middle of the building. It's an older building and the wear and tear shows. At least it looks clean. I cross to the balcony window and pull open the drapes. Nice view except for the filthy window. I can see out towards the harbor. I look down. I'm right above the pool; it's outside and atop a small out building to the side of the hotel with an elevated walkway from the third floor. Aww, when I had seen the pamphlet that said, "3rd floor pool," I assumed it was an indoor pool. Oh well. I unload the luggage trolley and set up the laptop. I was assured that I wouldn't hear the traffic. I hear it all. At least it isn't as annoying as previous places.

I'm hungry. I haven't eaten since 9 a.m. when I had a banana. The restaurant doesn't open until five. Wait, the lounge opens at three and as it's 4:30, I probably can hang around. I bet the views are wonderful. I take the trolley back to the lobby before heading to the top floor. The doors open onto a small area with the restaurant to the right and lounge on the left. I head into the lounge. Rows of floor to ceiling curved windows rim the outer edge.

My eyes are immediately drawn to one with that fabulous bridge in the far distance, the one I crossed earlier. It looks taller than any building in the city.

Rte. 17 through Charleston and the Arthur Ravenel, Jr. Bridge crossing the Cooper River

A Little Bridge History

The Arthur Ravenel Jr. Bridge crosses the Cooper River and was the second longest cable-stayed bridge in the Americas when it was built in 2005. There are eight lanes with a 12 foot lane for bicycles and pedestrians. The bridges it replaced were said to be two of the most dangerous in the United States.

The bartender is busy waiting on others. I put my notebook on a table and make my way from window to window checking the views and taking pictures. It is absolutely amazing. The windows form an arc about 180 degrees around the building. I figure the other half must be the kitchens. Every view is phenomenal. I stop back by the bar. Maybe I should get something special. I haven't had a real drink in a long time. I have no idea what to get. I ask for a rum punch. The bartender gives me a funny look. He says he supposes he can make one. Supposes? He shows me a drink menu. I order a Blue Carolinian, which is with Myers Dark Rum, Malibu Coconut Rum, Blue Curacao and pineapple juice.

It's now 5 p.m. so I head over to the restaurant side. I'm told I can sit anywhere and stop to chat with a couple. He is taking his wife out to dinner for her birthday. They've been married 50 years.

I choose a seat with a view of that fabulous bridge and order Caesar salad, prime rib, and garlic mashed. The prime rib is 50 percent fat, but the garlic mashed potatoes are delicious. I could eat a bowl of just that. I take my time enjoying the flavors and the awesome view. I don't care for the drink. It must be the Blue Curacao. I know I like rum and pineapple juice. The waitress suggests for the next one a Mai Tai. Oooohh, now that's good!

Darkness approaches and as the lights come on in the city I ask one of the waiters about lights on the big bridge. He tells me they keep lights dim because of turtles. I inquire about vending machines. The waitress says water in the lobby is more expensive than the vending machine on the 14th floor. Those rooms are meeting places and conference centers. I go the wrong way off the elevator and come almost all the way around the building before I find the vending area. The elevators really are the center of the building and all the rooms are along the outside. Going full circle makes me feel slightly light headed and I have a crazy notion to run all the way around like a child. At this stage of the game, I'd either pass out or throw up. (I kind of like the feeling.)

I can't wait to explore more.

DAY 7, SUNDAY, JANUARY 27

First Day in Charleston

I take my time this morning even though I'm up at my usual 5 a.m. It is nice to not feel I have to rush off today. I'm in the middle of my morning writing when it occurs to me that the sunrise from the restaurant on the 15th floor must be awesome. I throw on my clothes without showering because I know once dawn begins the sun rises quickly. Ah, just in time to get some nice photos. The views from these windows are stunning and there is enough cloud cover to make a spectacular sunrise. I take photos from most the windows to catch various angles until the sun's brilliance becomes blinding.

Pre-dawn view showing the curve of the restaurant.

I choose a table and settle in to have a real breakfast of buttermilk pancakes. Yum, they're good, fluffy, and great tasting. I can't eat them all. These are the most expensive pancakes I've ever had as I sign a $3 tip for the $11.59 bill. The views from this height are worth it. I'm able to sign with my room number and it will go on my credit card letting me save my cash. I take time over coffee and juice jotting down notes in my journal. I need this not-have-to-rush-off day even though I do want to do some sightseeing. The sunshine coming through the window is warm and soothing.

When more people begin coming in, I return to my room. I want to write the second installment to the day and import, edit, and upload photos to Facebook. I can't find my water bottle, so I drink more coffee. The computer is slow, the update to Flash Player won't install which means the photo uploads have to be done one at a time. How annoying. While waiting for each upload, I straighten out the clothes in my suitcases and organize by state all the brochures collected. (It feels like the pile weighs about 20 pounds.) By noon, my hands are shaking from too much coffee. I plan to take the 1:30 p.m. shuttle to the historic district and go for a carriage ride, but I better have lunch first. Maybe more food will stop the jitters. Look at me. I go days eating very little with only one meal a day then I make up for it by chowing down.

Buffet tables are lined with various foods. I help myself to chili, pineapple and cantaloupe chunks, pickled beets, rice, corn, string beans, and macaroni and cheese. I pass on the chicken wings, spare ribs, and beef stew. Oh, that food is so good. I'm not much of a chili eater, but this is excellent. The potato salad is wonderful. I could make a meal just of that. While eating, I add notations to my journal. My hand is so shaky it doesn't even look like my writing on the page. I go for a second helping and as I finish filling my plate, the guy comes over and says he'll be bringing desserts out shortly. Desserts? That's not going to happen.

I have just enough time to put my notebook back in the room, grab a sweater, and head to the lobby to get the shuttle. The hotel manager gives me a coupon for one of the carriage rides and I head outside to the van. It's an effort to maneuver the walking stick, camera, and get my short legs up that high. It feels good not to have to drive today. I can sit back, relax, and not worry about traffic or figure out where to go. The driver is talkative, and because I'm the only passenger, he brings me right to the carriage area instead of dropping me off at the designated stop a couple blocks away.

There are quite a few tour companies in this area. I don't even get a chance to look around before a woman immediately grabs my attention and I am letting her bring me to one. I'm buying the ticket before I realize this isn't the company for which I have the discount. Oops, too late now.

There's a 20-minute wait which gives me time to look around. The carriages are basically all the same with four benches. The driver stands. I'm disappointed to see how full the carriages are with four abreast on a seat. The thought of being squished in with strangers is not appealing. How am I going to take pictures? I chat with the woman signing people in when she isn't busy. We talk about the business, the horses, and being from the north (she's originally from northern Minnesota.) Taking the time to be friendly pays off because at boarding time, she puts me right up front in the corner with only two other people on the bench. That pleases me.

We are off and around the corner we make a stop. Because of the many carriage tour companies with each company having numerous carriages, the city set up a system to spread the carriages out so they are not all in the same areas. A bingo machine is used and the numbered ball that pops up is a designated route for that carriage. There is no favoritism and no choice. The carriage gets the route that comes up. The driver says it is possible that several rides would be needed to see all the sights as there's no guarantee that the next ride would be a different route. The drivers have no say in what they are given. It's all by chance. I would like to see the entire city, but can't see paying another $20 and end up seeing the same sights.

A Bit about the City

The old city of Charleston sits on a peninsula between the Ashley and Cooper Rivers. The Wando River flows into the Cooper just north of this area. All three rivers are tidal. Charleston is considered Low Country and the area frequently floods. In the early times, the English colony of Charles Town was plagued by attacks from Spanish, French, Indians, and pirates. Charleston was instrumental in the Revolutionary and Civil Wars. This was a trade city and ships were loaded with deer hides, indigo, tobacco, rice, and cotton. When slaves were brought to Charleston, they brought with them a vast knowledge of rice growing, which increased the wealth of plantation owners. This rice was known as Carolina Gold.

The architecture is fascinating. A lot of the houses are very narrow and tall. The guide explains the style is called the Charleston Single House. These are a single room across with a piazza on the south or west side. The main door is in the middle of the piazza. The door on the street is called a privacy door and when it's closed, it means the homeowners are not entertaining. In times past, when men often wore wool and women wore petticoats and other layers, it would be so hot that they'd strip down when they got home and would sit out on the piazzas in their underclothes. The closed privacy doors kept neighbors and others from wandering in. When the occupants were ready to have company, they'd open the door.

This city has frequent hurricanes and sometimes tornadoes. It also sits on the second largest fault in the country. In 1886, a 7.3 earthquake nearly destroyed the city. Summers are brutally humid and in the past, yellow fever was a major concern and more than once, the city was almost decimated by the disease.

The carriage meanders down narrow streets. Unfortunately, the ride is too bumpy to take photos or write down notes. The history and stories are fascinating and I hope I remember. The guide explains architecture unique to Charleston, customs, society and slavery of the past, and points out crepe myrtle trees. This is what I photographed yesterday thinking it was bark less. She says the bark is blonde and the tree usually has pink, yellow, or lavender flowers. The darker barked trees have white flowers. As we get closer to the waterfront, the wind coming off the harbor is quite cool. The couple sharing this bench has the seat blanket over their laps. I pull my sweater tighter. By the time the tour is over at 3:30, I am freezing. This is South Carolina, isn't it supposed to be warm? I want to return for another ride no matter what tour I get.

I need to be at the shuttle stop at 3:30 and I'm late. The next one won't be until 5:30. I have never done any type of tours like this, so I'm not sure of the protocols. I hobble to the corner not quite sure where to wait. This area has vendor stalls under huge canopies. I start to look around, but after the first few tables, nothing appeals to me. It's all tourist-type stuff. I go back outside wondering what to do until 5:30 and look up to see the Holiday Inn shuttle. I flag him down.

This guy isn't talkative like the first and again, I am the only passenger. He's friendly enough and answers when I ask periodic questions, but doesn't offer anything on his own. The stop where he picks me up is the first on his rounds, so I get to see more of the city. There's a specific set of stops they make every day and go around and around. I ask if he gets tired of the same old same old. He says he enjoys his job very much. The second stop is the Fort Sumter Visitor Education Center. The actual fort is an island accessible only by boat. The driver says this is where the Civil War started. That sounds like a plan for tomorrow.

An Evening on the 15th Floor

Back at the hotel, I decide I'm a little hungry. I'd had breakfast and lunch and don't need a big meal. On Sunday nights, they have a happy hour in the lounge until 8 p.m. with a buffet for $3.75. A buffet will work for me and I head up to the 15th floor. A DJ is setting up near the buffet table between the restaurant and lounge. I don't want to listen to loud music, so I follow the curve towards the back of the lounge. It will be quieter here. All the tables in the lounge are lined up in a single row along the floor-to-ceiling windows sitting four to a table. The last section is one step up, a wider more square area with four tables, two against the window and two against the opposite wall. The place is definitely more crowded than last night. I order a Mai Tai then check the buffet.

The table has a variety of cheeses, sliced ham and turkey, little cocktail wieners and meatballs, sliced tomato and that wonderful potato salad from lunch. I take some of the latter and a few meatballs and head back to my table. I open my notebook. It's hard to think of anything to write when the views out the window are so distracting.

The hotel's restaurant is open to the public and it's not long until almost every seat is taken. The two couples sitting at the table before mine are saying this is going to be their new hang out spot. This place would certainly be my hangout had I friends here with whom to hang out. Two more couples show up to join them and I offer to give up my spot which is bigger and will accommodate them more easily. They are grateful.

I move to the lower level and settle in the smaller space. For a few moments, melancholy settles over me. What would it be like to have good friends with whom to go out to enjoy music, food, and a couple drinks, especially at this time of night? Once more I feel I am on the outside looking in while others are having a great time. But I choose this life. I am not a party person, although I do enjoy people watching. I try to write a poem to match my mood. Like this hotel on the edge of the city, I feel I am present with the crowd and yet, I am not part of the action. As it is with me so often, I sit on the outskirts alone, just observing. It's as if I am in a bubble and time goes on around me and I am not allowed to participate.

Outskirts

On the outskirts of the city
rising high above other buildings
with breathtaking views
I sit alone in a crowded room

The babble of voices
and sounds of laughter
wrap in echoes around me
while night descends
in its cloak of navy blue

Far below, the Ashley River
winds its way past
highways and businesses
its sleepy waters
lapping gentle shores

I, too, on the outskirts
touch softly the gentle shores

What I like about this place, besides the view and the food, is that most
of these people are all, I would guess, over 40. Maybe the majority are even
over 55. Some are dressed well while others are more casual. The DJ is playing
blues. I keep looking out the window, watching the night advance, lights
come on over the city, dotted vehicle lights moving along the highways, and
waiting for the full moon to rise. I finish my meal, push the plate aside and
sip the Mai Tai as I write in my notebook. My foot is tapping to the music
when reflections moving in the windows catch my attention. I straighten up to
look more closely. What's going on? People are dancing! I watch, mesmerized,
although my only view is through the reflections in the curved glass. I'm
sitting too far away for a clear view of the actual dancers.

These are the older people and it looks like they are doing a kind of foxtrot
or cha-cha. I'm excited and impressed. It dawns on me that a lot of these
people know each other. How wonderful that people have a place to come
dance and still be early enough to be able to get home and in bed by 9 p.m. I

love that these are older couples. I watch them come up to the bar, some with walking sticks and canes, and soon they are out on the dance floor.

One of the women whom I'd given up my previous spot comes by and asks if I'm watching them, "doing the shag." She says to especially watch the guy with the white hair who is over 70. Shag? Is this a joke? The only shag term I've ever heard was a rug or . . . something we won't mention. She chuckles at my dumbfounded expression and explains that the shag is a dance unique to South Carolina. I still don't know if she's joking. Now I wish I was closer to the music. Or do I? Then I hear the bartender tell a patron that this is Sunday Night Shag Night and they do this almost every Sunday if there's nothing special going on; like next week which is Super Bowl Sunday. I try watching the dancers more closely from what I can see in the window reflections. Are they doing something like "Dirty Dancing?"

No, it really looks like cha-cha or foxtrot with the guy twirling his lady from time to time. This isn't modern dancing; the partners hold hands and are totally dancing with one another. I see the white-haired man the lady behind me pointed out. He really is a good dancer. There's even one tall, skinny, bent older man wearing a funny hat to everyone else's more "dressed up" look. He doesn't seem to be able to move a lot, but he is up there and dances with more than one woman. It seems they can do these steps to any song. The DJ is now playing a variety of songs, even more modern tunes. I guess the shag can be done to most any genre of music. What fun! I'm really impressed.

The camaraderie, laughter, and enjoyment are felt by everyone and there are smiles all around. I am even nodding my head and tapping foot or fingers to the music. How nice it is to hear other music. I'm getting tired of my CDs. This is one time I wish I had a partner who would dance with me. Still, I am totally enjoying this.

The wolf moon rises over the city of Charleston. I take a couple of photographs and head back to my room.

DAY 8, MONDAY, JANUARY 28

Ready for Another Day

It's Monday and I've been away from home for a full week. This is such an amazing journey. My emotions are all over the place. I was in such a hurry to get south that I wonder what I missed along the way. Should I have regrets? No, I can't allow those thoughts. I make decisions in the moment. The cold is definitely a factor in which places I visit. Plus, winters can be bleak. After awhile, all the dreariness looks the same. Had it been warmer, I might have made other decisions.

There's so much I want to see that it's hard to take the time to really enjoy one place. I want to go back into the historic part of the city, but don't know if I'll make the time. There are many other places to visit and Gail is looking forward to my spending a few days with her in Florida. I call the lobby to arrange to stay another night and let him know I need toilet paper. It's been good to be settled in one place for a couple of days. Don't feel like schlepping my stuff to another hotel and I do want to stay in Charleston for another couple of days. There is certainly good food here and it's great to not have to go out to get a decent meal.

The bill for the last two nights was slid under my door early this morning. Not only are they charging $89 per night, there's also a room tax of $12.02 per night, two destination fees at $1 each and two destination fee taxes at $.07 each. (Are the destination fees for the "free" shuttle service?)

I head up to breakfast to catch the sunrise. This is one way to make me eat in the morning. This time I choose a seat with a different view. It's quite overcast and I'm not sure I'll see the sun. I'm disappointed in the food. The bacon is cold, greasy, and horrible. Whoever thought bacon could be bad. The waitress isn't friendly. She shuffles along like she doesn't want to be here. The hostess is nice, though. The sun doesn't actually show until it is high and bright. I still take photos of the fabulous view and return to my room to find two rolls of toilet paper on my suitcase. Guess I'll have to put them on the spindles myself. Not a big deal.

I want make some observations about hotels. Most of the places I've stayed have a small refrigerator, microwave, coffee maker, and internet. This place does not have a microwave. Is that to get you to do room service or visit the restaurant? The bathroom vanity is small and with the coffee maker on it, doesn't leave much room for personal items.

Commentary on Bathrooms

I get a chuckle over bathrooms. In two of the rooms where I stayed, the toilet paper dispenser was on the back wall next to the tank. I'm short with short arms and there are issues with my back so I have to be careful when twisting. In two other rooms, the dispenser was to the right, but level with the tank, so it was still a reach around, and in yet another room, the dispenser was right by the knee. Being a little on the wide side, getting paper off the roll is a little tight.

In other bathrooms, the dispenser is closer to the floor and which entails bending over to reach the paper (and when I have to bend over, it's low.) Then care needs to be taken to keep the paper off the floor as it is being pulled from the roll. In some bathrooms, space is often so cramped that one has to squeeze between the toilet and wall to get the door closed. That's a big "ewww."

Last year I had installed comfort height toilets at the house and the hotels all have regular ones. I now realize what my mom used to complain about in trying to get off the seat. I may have short legs, but with bad knees getting up from a lower position is not easy. Who came up with these designs and does anyone else find this curious?

I also wonder about faucets. The sink is usually a nice round bowl, but the faucet is often short. I have to reach to the back of the bowl to get my hands wet. Sometimes I end up touching the back of the sink and in some places that can be gross. Plus water splashes all over the back to the wall. There are brands of faucets with taller necked faucets, but the curve is still the same.

A couple restaurants I've visited have had their restrooms renovated with the new vessel sinks made to sit on top of the counter. These beautifully created bowls made of glass, stone, ceramic, porcelain, brass, or copper are works of art. However, it's difficult for shorter people to wash their hands. Depending on the size and style, I usually have to stand on tip toe to reach over the rim of the bowl and it's not comfortable.

I take a break from my writing and look out the window. Oh, the sun is going to peek over the clouds. There are white birds with black-tipped wings. I can't tell if they are terns or some kind of southern sea gull. I'm debating about the boat ride to Fort Sumter.

On to Fort Sumter

I decide not to drive again today. The hotel's shuttle will drop me off at the museum where I'll pick up the boat. There was a brief glimpse of the sun earlier, but it slipped behind the clouds. I am a little leery about going out on the water with the morning being overcast and windy. I can't find my gloves and search the truck when I go out after my coat. The morning is cool and it doesn't look like the overcast will break. I hope the boat ride through the harbor to the island won't be too cold. Josh, from the front desk, is the shuttle driver for the morning run. He drops some people off at MUSC, which I find out does not stand for music, but Medical University of South Carolina. I am the last drop off at the Fort Sumter Museum. He tells me to be here for pick up at 1:30 as the next shuttle won't be until 3:30 p.m.

There is a steep, tall set of stairs to climb and I'd forgotten to take pain reliever before I left. Good thing I brought my walking stick. I make my way slowly up the steps and buy a ticket for $18. There's an hour to wait. I wander through the museum reading about the events leading up to the Civil War, South Carolina history, slave trade, and Fort Sumter and the surrounding forts. Reading about slavery gives me a sick feeling in the pit of my stomach. Just the thought that people were sold and treated like animals or worse is so wrong.

I meander outside and take photos of that bridge that has me fascinated and try to get pictures of the porpoise and pelican. It's a two-flight stairway down to board the boat. I am very slow on stairs and let others go around me. Most people go below deck to be out of the wind, but I opt to be among the few to stay topside. It's half an hour out to the island. Yes, it's cold, but not horribly so. Many people have scarves, hats, gloves, and hoods pulled up and tied tight.

A Little History

Charleston has an amazing history. This city has the largest container port on the east coast and in the early days, it was a major port in the slave trade. Sullivan Island was where most all the slaves first came when brought to America. Everyone coming into Charleston who couldn't prove to be free of disease was quarantined on the island for a couple weeks or more. Thousands upon thousands of slaves were brought there before being sold.

Forts were built on many of the islands around Charleston Harbor. (Most are now accessed by roads. Yeah, those bridges that have me so intrigued.) Fort Sumter was built after the War of 1812 in the middle of harbor making it a strategic location for defense of the city. The five-sided brick edifice originally had three tiers and by the start of the Civil War, still wasn't completely finished.

When South Carolina seceded from the Union, Union forces were occupying Fort Sumter. The North refused to vacate beginning a two-day bombardment. The South then held the fort from mid April 1861 to mid February 1865 experiencing the longest siege in modern warfare. By then, the top two tiers were destroyed and the fort in ruins. Following the war, the fort was used as an unmanned light house station, but as the Spanish-American War began, fortifications were made. A huge concrete emplacement was built in 1898 and painted black.

Visitors disembark the boat and walk down a long pier to the entrance. Passing through the sally port I see familiar brick work and cannon like in the forts along New Hampshire and Maine. The group moves into the courtyard. To the left and right are the brick fortifications one would see in an old fort, but straight across is something out of the Twilight Zone. We all stare. It looks like the top of a huge black battleship. This is totally unexpected. There wasn't any way to tell from the outside that something like this was here. It's fascinating and yet, unsettling. My first thought is "This doesn't belong here."

Painted Black

A park ranger offers a guided tour. I hear him explaining that updates were done during WWII to make the fort difficult to be detected by U-boats and that part of the fort was painted black to make it look like a war ship. The black walls and roofs are weird; the dark color, texture, and age are such a contrast to the old red bricks of the other walls.

I wander off on my own to take a lot of photos. I enjoy the older sections; places that used to be rooms, barracks, kitchens, gun placements, and explore a narrow brick corridor leading outside where I watch porpoises and sea birds. Back inside the fort, I climb many, many steps to the rampart. The sun peeks out a bit. I am hot and had forgotten that even under cloudy skies, one can get sunburn. I feel it in my face. I take pictures around the upper levels and slowly make my way back down those stairs, one painful step at a time. I don't bother to look in the museum or gift shop because I don't want to carry anything on the boat. I'll get something back at the other museum on the mainland.

I'm one of the first back on the boat. I forgot that the smell of diesel makes me nauseous. Needless to say, I don't enjoy the ride back as much as the ride out. However, I do get some more photos of that fascinating bridge and the USS Yorktown. The aircraft carrier towers over the pier and small building on the right.

A Little More History

The USS Yorktown is an aircraft carrier turned museum. It was built similar to the USS Yorktown that was sunk at Pearl Harbor and given the same name. That previous one was a CV5and this one a CV7. The last duty this ship had was to retrieve Apollo 7 after its splashdown from the journey into space. The ship is now docked at Patriots Point.

We get back to the mainland a little after 1 p.m. I want to get postcards, but my legs will not take any more stairs and the elevator is out of order. I waddle out front to wait for the shuttle. Oh, I ache. A couple guys from Ohio start a conversation. Well, one guy talks while the other studies a map. They are on their way over to Patriots Point. It's nice to have a relaxing conversation. Most of the people I've talked to on this trip have been working, so it's hard to really get into anything.

They leave and I sit on the bench to wait . . . and wait. Am I in the right place? I get out the little map which shows the stops. This looks right. I get up and walk out to an area where I see a bus drop off people. No, I know I wasn't dropped off here and return to the bench. I'll wait until 2 p.m. then try to find a taxi.

Josh finally rounds the bend, all apologetic. He'd been held up by a train. There is another passenger from this morning and the three of us have a great conversation. I'm confused about tipping. A person could go broke with everyone to tip. I had given Josh $5 earlier. I have no idea if that was too little or too much, but when I notice my fellow passenger only give $1, I figure what I gave earlier covered both rides.

Unfortunately, by the time I get back to the hotel, I've missed lunch. Drat! That means I have to wait until 5 p.m. It's just as well. I need the rest. I climbed so many stairs today; one flight to the museum, two flights down to the loading dock, three flights up at the fort and back down again. That doesn't count all the standing around waiting, standing on the boat and all the other walking, ramps, inclines and such. I can use the time to import photos from the past two days, edit some, and post those onto Facebook. Karen messages to say that Freyja is under the covers, the water is running, and she turned down the heat. I always feel better hearing things are okay on the home front. I miss my fur ball.

I go up to the restaurant for dinner. This is my favorite place to be. It's a beautiful evening with spectacular views. I remember to tell the waiter "light on the dressing" for my Caesar salad. It's gorgeous up here after dark with dots of lights all over the city. It's nice to be in the city and yet away from all the hustle and bustle. I'm sleepy. The Mai Tai is delicious. I could get used to this.

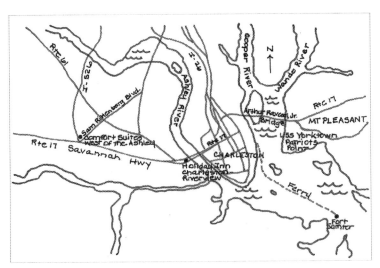

Old City and Fort Sumter

DAY 9, TUESDAY, JANUARY 29

Goodbye Holiday Inn

Noisy neighbors wake me about 2:30 a.m. slamming doors and yelling, then again at 3:30, and 4 a.m. I finally get up at 4:30 and I can still hear them yakking. Not sure if they are arguing or just enjoying themselves. There is a Do Not Disturb sign on their doorknob when I go out to go to breakfast at 7 a.m. I am tempted to re-open and slam my door a few times.

I am looking forward to a beautiful sunrise and I'm shocked to come around the corner from the elevator to find there is absolutely no view out the windows. Has someone pulled the shades? Then it dawns on me it is thick fog. I look out a window. I can just barely make out cars crossing the bridge. I pity people driving to work in this and try to imagine what this tower would be like during a storm. Do they evacuate during hurricanes? Oooh, scary.

Breakfast is disappointing; thick and dense like the fog outside and tasteless. When the waiter asks if I need anything else, I almost ask for a steak knife to cut the rubber pancakes. The flavor is there once I chew for a bit. I eat about half and a few pieces of fruit. By the time I am ready to leave, a faded sun has risen over the fog bank. It's creating a weird light over the landscape.

I plan on going to Magnolia Plantation and Gardens. It's a 500-acre estate with walking and bike trails, nature train, boat tour, and more. That should keep me busy today. It's touted as being "One of the top 25 most visited historic houses in America" and one of the "most beautiful gardens in the world." I take my usual three pain killers, pack up and load the luggage trolley. Well, I suppose I should get to it. I'm done with this place.

I check out of the Holiday Inn Riverview before 9 a.m. The temperature is 55 degrees and the fog has lessened. I wipe the moisture off the sides and back window after putting the luggage in the truck. No matter which way I go to leave the hotel, I am pulling onto the left lane of a three-lane highway. To go towards the plantations is a left out of the parking lot onto Rte. 17S and quickly crossing the three lanes to take an almost immediate right on Rte. 61. I go to the far end of the lot and wait for a break in the heavy traffic. It's not easy to keep an eye out for a chance to cross three lanes. The lady behind the desk had told me to just be patient and finally there's an opening and I scoot across.

Route 61 is another three-lane divided highway with periodic stoplights for those needing to exit or enter. Stop and go, stop and go. At one point Rte. 61 curves to the left and Rte. 171 to the right. I pull in to the Rite Aid in the fork to get a couple bottles of water. My little discount tag I use back home works here. Further along, construction causes a little anxiety. More lanes are being added. It's hard for me to imagine so much traffic everywhere that all the roads need to be six lanes, three in each direction and that's not counting turn lanes. Sometimes signs are displaced or equipment is in the way. I keep an eye out for workers and other travelers. It must be difficult for businesses to have all this construction blocking access.

Ah, there's a sign pointing left. Oh, this road is more like it. It's a simple two lanes and the landscape opens up into more residential, golf course, school, and trees begin to reach high over the road creating a canopy.

There are three plantation areas along this route; Drayton Hall, Magnolia Plantation and Gardens, and Middleton Place. I pass Drayton Hall which cannot be seen from the road, but a place I plan to visit before I leave Charleston. I'm starting with Magnolia, which is the middle one. From what I see of the brochure, I want to spend the most time here.

Morning at Magnolia Plantation and Gardens

I pull in past the sign to follow a long paved driveway lined with trees, vines, and other vegetation. The way winds past palmettos and swampy looking ponds. Graveled paths big enough for golf carts occasionally cross the road. There are sections where the trees and brush look newer. I wonder if this was part of plantation fields in by-gone days and now without the hand of man keeping the land clear, nature reclaims its own.

As I park, there's a big clock on the ground which looks like it might have been part of a steeple. It says 9:38 a.m. I put on my sweater with its big pockets so pens, pad of paper, and reading glasses fit along with the keys. At the ticket booth, I say I want to do everything. There are nature and bike paths, petting zoos, Nature Train, House Tour, Freedom to Slavery Tour, and a Nature Boat. Unfortunately, the boat doesn't run in the winter. The lady says that I can park at the swamp and walk the boardwalks on the way out.

I purchase the garden tour, train ride, house tour, slave cabins talk, and swamp walk. The ticket is good for two days. There's about half an hour before the Nature Train, so I explore the nearby area. Quite a few people are working the grounds. It must take a lot to maintain the 500 acres, though I don't know how much of that acreage is wetland. I ask one of the guys about the trees with the moss. Come to find out, they ARE oak trees! No one knows if they are related to our oaks in the north. The leaves are so different from the red and white oaks back home. These remind me of rhododendron leaves.

The Nature Train is not a real train, but a couple of cars pulled by a Clark (reminds me of the old Clark fork trucks we had at work years ago, minus the forks.) The tour goes around the perimeter of the property. The road is bumpy, so I can't take notes as the driver points out blue-winged teal, coots, rails, green-winged teals, egrets, great blue herons, and a bald eagle. He also talks about the oak trees calling them Virginia live oak. This is not an evergreen tree. Leaves drop from January to March, but before they do, the new leaves come in so the tree always has foliage. Some of these trees are over 400 years old and they are massive.

Magnolia Gardens is the oldest public garden in the U.S. and is on the National Register of Historic Places. It was the first plantation to be open to tourists. (The family had fallen on hard times and needed money.) The guide points out other plants. There are over 200 species of azaleas on the property. Wherever the name of the plant is mentioned, it is given its Latin name because of the number of varieties of each. Many plants were imported. The wealthy planters gathered species from all over the world. There are lots of knobby trunk growths along the waterways. He calls them cypress knees and they grow up from the roots of trees. They remind me of gnomes, a bunch of gnomes at a party.

Unfortunately, we are going too fast to get a lot of photos and although there are a couple stops, we aren't allowed to get off the car. The ponds and ditches are full of duck weed which looks like thick green algae. I almost think it could be walked on until I get a closer view. Lots of birds and other creatures feed on this weed. He says this is a slow season, that often these waters are full of fowl. There are turtles and I see my first alligator. "It's still a little too cold for alligators," he says.

It's Too Cold for Alligators

All the ditches were dug by slaves for irrigation. The original owners of this plantation made their fortune on rice. Rice was one of the major staples of South Carolina along with cotton, indigo, and tobacco. I am totally surprised by that. I never realized that rice was a big production in the states. Growing rice is very labor intensive which is why there is not much of an industry in it now. Rice needs to be planted and harvested by hand. Because of the need for so much water, heavy equipment cannot be used due to the softness of the land.

The train drops us at the house where the next tour begins. This was the third building on the site. The original burned down from a lightning strike and the second destroyed by union soldiers. This house was constructed using phosphate mixed with lime and water and reminds me of stucco. It's a little more stable than wood. The texture is very rough. I like it, but others think it ugly.

We go up a flight of stone steps for the beginning of the tour. The first floors of most homes around Charleston are elevated because the area is low country and frequently floods. This means there are no basements like we have back home. Humidity is tremendously high and mosquitoes cause malaria. (The other day I was giving the impression that the mosquitoes here are like small aircraft carriers.) The wealthy of years past often had other homes to go to during the summer either on the coast or up in the mountains.

Brief History about Magnolia Plantation

This property was first developed by Thomas Drayton in 1679. Like many of the early plantation owners he was originally from England, had properties in Barbados, and came here when King Charles offered land grants. Members of the Drayton family have owned Magnolia for more than 300 years. This place saw the wealth and growth from rice; both British and American troops occupied the property during the American Revolution. Drayton's sons were statesmen and soldiers fighting for the freedom of this country. The gardens continued to be expanded throughout the centuries with influences from French and English gardens.

John Grimké Drayton introduced the first azaleas to America and was the first to use Camellia Japonica outdoors. Today there are multiple gardens and paths lined with many varieties of these species. After the Civil War, rice production declined, but the gardens continued to be expanded and later became the major focus of the property.

Afternoon at Magnolia

After the house tour, I have an hour before the slave talk. I buy a cheeseburger and a bottle of water then take a walk along the Ashley River, which was the major mode of transportation to Charleston back in the day. By buggy, it was a six-hour drive, but by boat, only two hours. Plantation houses were built facing the river with the carriage driveway coming up to the back.

Garden Path Along the Ashley River

It's gorgeous along these trails. On one side, giant live oaks with long clumps of Spanish moss hanging from limbs line sections of the shoreline while on the other side there are beautiful camellias in reds, whites, and a couple shades of pink. These shrubs are taller than I with the upper branches on both sides of the walkway meeting overhead to form tunnel-like corridors. The blossoms turn brown on the edges and drop to the ground making colorful walkways.

I'm hot and make my way back to the truck, take off that heavy sweater, and squeeze a smaller notebook, pens, and reading glasses into my pants pockets. A bench in the shade is a good place to await the next tour. I want to take some notes from what I've seen and learned so far, but my poor brain will not recall anything. Instead, I get into a conversation with a woman from New York. We talk about the oak trees and she agrees with me. She is also traveling alone, so we sit together on the train as it takes us to a set of slave cabins. Our guide is a young woman who leads us over to a set of picnic tables to explain slavery in the U.S. and how it came to be. I am in the beginning of the group, but step back saying that I would let all the younger people go first as I am so slow.

"What younger people?" one of the others exclaims and when I look around, we are all up there in years. I'm not the only one using a walking stick. Everyone chuckles.

A Very Brief Lesson in Slavery

Sarah says that in the beginning, slaves were not kidnap victims from Africa for the slave trade in America. It started with African tribal wars and the winning warriors trading captives to the Europeans. The Europeans brought the Africans to America. As plantations grew and more slaves needed, the abductions and selling became more brutal.

As she tells her stories, her voice chokes and her eyes fill with tears. Here is a young white woman who really feels for these people and the horrid conditions they were subjected to. Oftentimes, on the trip across the Atlantic, they were chained, lying down and packed like sardines, only being allowed up once a day. They slept, urinated, and defecated in that same spot. Many died. Some jumped overboard the minute they had a chance figuring that at least in suicide, they'd be free and their souls could return home.

Once the ship reached Charleston, it was quarantined sometimes for up to three months to make sure the slaves were free of disease. At this point, they were given good food to fatten them up for sale. Any with gray hair had charcoal rubbed in so the gray wouldn't show to the buyers. The bodies would often be oiled to better define muscles. Planters, what the plantation owners were called, wanted strong bodies to work their fields.

The homes that the slaves were given were often one small room for an entire family and there wasn't any insulation. All cooking was down outside because of fire hazards. It was against the law for them to sleep outside, so even in the high humidity they had to sleep in those cramped little rooms.

But in spite of all that, they brought a culture and expertise to this new land that allowed them to survive. It was their knowledge that made plantations successful. They knew land, knew how to cultivate and care for it and its crops. These people may have been uneducated by white standards (or at least that's what those in power wanted everyone to believe) but they were far from ignorant. They had their community and continued their heritage through story and song.

Many of these "slave quarters" were for two families. The swamp is directly behind the buildings which was at one time the rice fields. Alligators and snakes were a danger and the only weapons the slaves had to defend themselves were sharpened sticks. I couldn't imagine living that close to where something could crawl out of the bushes and kill me. Plus there were mosquitoes, gnats, and lots of other nasty crawly things that could cause sickness or death.

At the end of that tour, I again get off the train at the house. I want to check out an area that I noticed earlier.

Red Bridge Reflections

Sasha Wolfe

I take a trail down by the river. I cross bridges and keep telling myself that I'll go "just a little further." I want to see an eagle. No such luck. I do see a couple little alligators and lots of coots and teal. Finally, I turn around and head back. There's still so much to see, but I'm dragging.

Crossing Bridges

I learned so much and wish I could have taken notes. I cannot remember all I heard. It's so fascinating. Life down here was so different from up north because of the landscape and weather. What I remember from history books at school cannot compare to actually being in the physical location and hearing stories told from a more personal view. The heroes from early American history had a darker side. Many of the founding fathers and those instrumental in the nation's liberty were slave owners. They fought for freedom from British rule and yet, believed they had the right to "own" others. Their beliefs were only for white men just like themselves.

For some, the subject of slavery is hard to talk about to this day. Even after the Civil War, the belief continued that the wealthy white society was above everyone else. The slaves may have been "freed," but they were still given very few rights and that continued into the 20th century. My mind is overwhelmed and some of these tales are disturbing. I'm not sure what to think, only that more of the "real" truth needs to be brought forth.

I stop at the ticket booth on the way out to ask about returning tomorrow. She says I must check in and get a new stamp, but today's fees will cover that visit. I ask about a Comfort Suite Inn and she gives directions back towards town, but not taking Rte. 61 all the way to Rte. 17. She says to take Bees Ferry Road to Glen McConnell Parkway and get on Rte. 526 which will bring me out at Savannah Highway, which is Rte. 17. The hotel is right at the intersection.

I drive back towards the city and find the hotel. It's 72 degrees. Finally some warmth! The odometer reads 14,458.3 which means I've driven 1,292.2 miles since leaving home. I'll stay here for a couple days. I'm not done with Charleston yet.

The Comfort Suites West of the Ashley is cheaper than the Holiday Inn, has a nicer, newer room, a much better bathroom, and there's an indoor pool. Room 117 is on the highway side. Thankfully, the noise does not permeate the walls that badly. I've got to remember to ask for a room away from the highway, though in this case it wouldn't matter as the Sam Rittenberg Highway, Rte. 7, is on the other side.

I settle in by 4:30, put on my swimsuit and head for the pool. Oh, this feels good after a long day. I do my usual 20 minutes or more constantly moving and not touching bottom. I order take out when I'm back in the room. Already I miss the restaurant and the fabulous views, but enjoy chicken fingers and a Caesar salad while watching TV. Today was the most distance I've walked in a long time. I call it an early night.

DAY 10, WEDNESDAY, JANUARY, 30

A Plan to Return

Day 10 on the road. I'm beginning to lose track of time and what day it is even though I write every day. The lady at Magnolia Gardens had told me that I should return in the morning because rain is expected in the afternoon. Now that it's daylight, it is quite overcast. I want to hang out here a bit and do some writing, but perhaps I should take off soon and come back early. Maybe I'll only do the part of Magnolia I missed yesterday and save the other two places until tomorrow.

Gosh, I'm getting old! I can't handle more than one thing in a day. I'm repeating myself more, too. Yesterday was a long day of walking around. Needless to say, my legs and feet are still hurting. Maybe I'll take four pain relievers today instead of my usual three. This is all so fascinating. I know I keep saying this, but I love Charleston, except for the freeways. There is so much traffic. I am amazed that although my room is right next to the highway, it's not that bad.

I finish writing about yesterday and now I'm ready to head out. I went out to the truck earlier. They said it is 70 degrees, but it doesn't feel it. There's quite a breeze and it's overcast. I like it. Maybe I won't be as hot walking as I was yesterday.

I buy two bottles of water and get directions back to Magnolia. With divided highways and right and left exits, I easily get confused. I have to take a right out of the parking lot and take an immediate right onto Sam Rittenberg Boulevard which comes around the back of the hotel. I'm surprised there is not direct access from the parking lot. The boulevard is another stop and go, light after light, store after store area. I get gas at a Sunoco station, $3.27/gal. I pick up Rte. 61N and retrace yesterday's drive.

Magnolia Revisited

At Magnolia Plantation, I am given a new sticker. I explore the petting zoo taking photos of turkeys, peacocks, and other birds. They have an albino raccoon. I debate what else to do. I saw most of everything here yesterday, so I get in the truck and drive to the Audubon Swamp Garden which is part of the plantation.

My legs are stiff and I'm moving slowly as I get out of the truck. Not a big deal. There isn't anyone else around. There's a short walk through a mucky area to the entrance and a few steps up to the platform which faces a big stockade fence. A security code is needed to gain access. The eight-foot-tall, heavy wooden gate swings slowly open and I wonder, once I enter, if I'll be able to get back out.

This is a beautiful boardwalk out over the swamp. Much of the water is covered in a thick green slime called duck weed, which is one of the world's smallest flowering plants. Yesterday's tour guide had talked about it and now I see it up close. It's free floating, seed bearing, and each frond is approximately 1/16 of an inch. Duck weed filters water to keep it clean and because of its abundance, it makes a great wintering place for many varieties of birds. There are hundreds of water fowl; different types of teal, coots, and ducks along with ibis, snowy egrets, great egrets, green herons, and great blue herons. A turtle crawls up on a log covered in the green sludge. I take many pictures before I get a few feet.

Covered in Duckweed

As I am wont to do, I try to walk softly which is not easy on wood. I don't want to scare any of the wildlife plus I just like to be quiet. My mind is assailed by sights that I don't normally see and there's constant chatter in my head, "Look at that" and "that" and "What are those birds?" There's no one to voice it aloud to, though. I am alone; just my camera and I.

At an intersection, I stay to the right to take the Swamp Trail. Where there is dry land, the boardwalk gives way to dirt paths. Some walkways slant and for others there are a couple of steps. I stop often for photographs and to watch the birds and admire the scenery. The wind whips my jacket and blows my hair. For the longest time, I am the only human around. It is so peaceful. Suddenly another person jogs into view. It's the young woman who had given the talk on slavery yesterday. We say hello and I tell her that I enjoyed her talk as she runs on by. I am alone once more. I would have liked a little conversation.

In the distance against a gray sky, I see dark clumps in the upper branches of trees. Are those nests? I put the camera to my eye and extend the lens. Oh, my, gosh, not only nests, but there are great blue herons in those trees. I can't believe how anything that big can build nests in branches so high and thin. There has to be eight to ten nests in that one tree and almost all the nests have a heron in it. Back home I only see single birds and here there are many.

Herons at Nest

In the swamps, two major trees grow; tupelo and cypress. From a poster, I learn a little more about the Spanish moss. It's an epiphyte which means it gathers nutrients from the air and rain water and does not harm the trees. So many things that were just words now I am given a visual. It's mind-boggling. Part of me wants to stop and study while the other part of me wants to hurry on to see what else there is to discover. I take pictures of the information signs. I can do the reading up later.

I learn the difference between some of the birds: great egrets – yellow bills and black legs; snowy egrets – black bills and legs; great white heron – yellow bills and legs; white ibis – decurved red bill, face, and legs; and glossy ibis – decurved dark bill and legs.

It is funny to see an occasional narcissus in bloom on patches of dry land where the only other color is the bright green of saw palmetto; one bright spot of yellow in a dull winter landscape. I try to envision what summers would look like when leaves are full and more flowers in bloom. I'm sure I wouldn't like the heat and humidity.

There are quite a few yellow bellied sliders and I get a glimpse of one alligator. The walk is so peaceful even though I am aching. There only sounds are of the wind whooshing through trees and swamp grass and the various calls of birds. Magnolia Plantation is near the Charleston Airport and an air force base, so occasionally a big plane flies overhead. I want to know the names of the plants. I can only rely on the info signs that are few and far between.

The Swamp Trail makes a long U-shape from the entrance off the exit road near a private area and comes out on the other side of the large swamp. From there, I take the High Ridge loop which cuts back through the middle of the swamp. I stop at a couple of look-out areas. My eyes see things for which my mind has no words. I am awed and fascinated.

This was supposed to be a 45-minute walk, but I take my time and two hours go by before I feel the urge to leave. I come across a noisy family and step aside to let them pass. I wish parents would teach their children to be quiet in natural settings. I am reminded of the times I brought my grandchildren on nature hikes. They were so excited. We'd practice being quiet in hopes of seeing deer or chipmunks. I enjoyed sharing that experience and they were so appreciative. I still feel that excitement when I am out in nature.

I've had enough for one day. I consider visiting Drayton Hall, but my legs and feet won't take it. It's time to head back to the city. As I reach the gate, I wonder how to operate it from this side when it swings open. More people are arriving just in time for me to slip through.

Magnolia Plantation and Gardens is a must-see destination for anyone visiting South Carolina. I could easily spend days wandering the trails and most are handicapped accessible. This place must be amazing in full color. I'd love to see the wisteria in bloom. The camellia is in bloom, but most are going by and many blossoms lie on the ground. Visitors can purchase one of the shrubs. If I was going home now, I'd buy one (after making sure it would grow in the north.)

I stop at a Hardees Restaurant on Rte. 17N for lunch, which is on the wrong side from the hotel. The food is just okay and trying to get back to the Comfort Suites, I have to find a set of lights to be able to switch directions. The first turn I make doesn't work and I get back on 17N going past the hotel. I am finally able to make a left into a store parking lot where I can turn around and get on 17S to the hotel.

Back at the hotel, I take a nap. I ache. I'm still tired. The traveling is taking its toll. Later, I take a quick swim before hitting the books. I'm getting confused with the days and go back over the journal entries to get the time lines correct. I also import and edit some of the photos taken at Magnolia Plantation and Gardens. What an amazing place. That's a place I'd like to return to sometime. Facebook is giving me a hard time uploading the photos. Some days it works so quickly and others are a nightmare.

I feel guilty for not doing any drawing. I consider it, but it's too much of an effort to drag the easel and materials in from the truck. Yes, it's been too cold to set up en plein air, but I have photos from which I could work. I could draw in the sketch book and not set up the easel, but all the supplies are packed in the easel case. Maybe the next time I take a trip, I'll pack easily accessible drawing supplies. I just can't get into it right now. I'm too busy seeing all that I can see, taking photos, and writing.

I order chicken tenders and Caesar salad and settle in to watch "American Pickers" and "Storage Wars." I flip back and forth during commercials. I crawl into bed at my usual time.

DAY 11, THURSDAY, JANUARY 31

Editing Photos

I am up at 4 a.m. and finish uploading photos of my visit to Magnolia Plantation and Gardens. Facebook is being slow and they have to be done one at a time. Last night's blog is finished. I'm struggling with feeling disorganized. I had planned on keeping everything in order and I wanted to keep an accurate daily record of all doings. Somehow, I got mixed up. My poor brain short circuits. Can I blame it on age? I've notes written in four different notebooks.

It's very different down here. To get to a place on the other side of the road, I have to drive in the opposite direction to turn around and come back because of the divided highways. Sometimes I take an exit expecting to turn into a place only to find myself on another highway in which I have to drive a bit to find where to turn around to come back. Sometimes there are left turns and sometimes I have to go right to get to the left and many times I don't know where the turn is until I'm there. I drive in the middle lane and hope that when I see which exit I want, the traffic will let me in.

It's confusing and overwhelming. I'm not used to it. The extra thinking tires me out. Okay, maybe getting up at 4-4:30 every morning doesn't help. Still, I want to get writing done. By 5 or 6 p.m., my brain is too fried to concentrate. I'm not able to work at night.

Today I will tell the front desk that I'll stay at least one more night, maybe two. There's Middleton Place and Drayton Hall to visit, which are on my agenda today. I'm not sure I can fit in both in one day. That's not counting Cypress Gardens (the one in South Carolina, not Florida.) Plus it's getting towards the end of the week and I need to consider my newspaper work.

It's close to 8 a.m. The sun is shining and the sky looks clear. From what I see of Middleton Place information, it must be quite large. It boasts an inn and restaurant. I'll go there first after I clean up here a bit and put away papers and receipts I no longer need. I'll head out about 9 a.m.

Middleton Place

I don't check the weather before leaving this morning and because yesterday was 78 degrees, I'm not wearing a turtleneck. The temperature is only 50 degrees and it's windy. I get to the Middleton Place at 9:30. Luckily, I'd left a sweater and coat in the truck and I need both. As a matter of fact, I even do up the top two buttons on the coat to protect my neck.

I pay the fee at the ticket booth; $48 covers entrance, African American Focus Tour and Carriage Ride. There are no house tours today nor is the restaurant open; just my luck. Oh, well. I am given a map and stuff it in a pocket. First up, the carriage ride in which I am the only passenger. They have a blanket on the bench which I gratefully put over my lap. The history of these areas is so fascinating and the tour guides are great. The carriage bumps over muddy paths through 20-foot-tall bamboo. Wow, that's tall. She says that it now grows wild and they use if for barricades. Again, the ride is too bumpy to take many photographs or to take notes. Between the carriage ride and the slavery tour, I piece together the story as well as I can remember:

Middleton History

Two Middleton brothers came to America from Barbados. The family was originally from England. They wanted to build plantations like in Barbados, yet be English aristocracy. Their empire grew as they acquired more land through grants from the king. Henry Middleton acquired the current property through his marriage to Mary Williams. Timber, hunting for hides, and cattle were the earliest commodities to sell. There were about 7,000 acres to this property although the family owned many other places. Henry Middleton set out to create an immense garden and slaves were put to work under the instruction of an English landscaper.

Along with sugar cane from Barbados, rice was brought from Madagascar. At first, an experiment, rice turned out to be the crop to bring fortune and this was all possible because of the labor of slaves. Indentured servants did not work out because they could not take the humidity and the hard physical labor. Native Americans did not work out as slaves because they could easily disappear into the familiar countryside.

African slaves were originally the booty of warring nations with the winning kings or tribal leaders trading them to the Europeans for supplies and goods. Charleston was the major port in America. Some of the slaves brought to America were highly skilled; carpenters, masons, seamstresses, and more, and it was through the African culture that the rice plantations became so profitable for the planters.

Middleton slaves worked on a task system. A slave was assigned a task for the day and when that task was done, the day was done and he/she could go "home." The work day was Monday through Friday with a half day on Saturday and Sundays off. Each family was allowed a little plot to have a garden of their own. Slaves generally ate well-balanced meals because it was important to keep them healthy and strong.

By the time of the Revolutionary War, Arthur Middleton, later a signer of the Declaration of Independence, was a staunch supporter for American liberty and when the British stormed up from Savannah, Middleton was imprisoned in St. Augustine. The British ransacked the mansion. Middleton returned to rebuild.

The Civil War was devastating to plantation owners. Union soldiers overtook Middleton Place and destroyed most everything, burning the main house and north flanker. (Flankers were adjacent buildings not attached to the Big House and often contained guest quarters, kitchens, or music rooms.) Soldiers also demolished the slaves' homes. The odd thing is that they never touched the chapel or the rice mill building. Those are still standing today.

With the freeing of the slaves and with no one left to tend the fields, the days of plantations were over. Some rebuilding went on and some former slaves came back to work for the Middletons. Just because slaves were "free," that didn't permit them acceptance or jobs. They were still poor, they were still uneducated (by American standards) and they were still considered barbarians; in other words, they were free in name only.

In 1886, the Great Earthquake shook the countryside. It is said it would have registered 7.3 on the Richter scale. What remained of the big house and north flanker was totally destroyed and the property was left to go wild for a many years.

Today, this part of the property, once over 7,000 acres, consists of 110 acres of sculptured lawns, gardens, and restored outbuildings. One thing that impresses me is that a lot of the fencing and some of the outbuildings were made from the bricks from the destroyed buildings.

Oh, I could go on, but this is not a history lesson . . . well, maybe for me. After my one-person tour, I wander around on my own. The house and restaurant are closed for renovations, but there is plenty to see. I visit the stable area where there are not only barnyard animals, but also peacocks and water buffalo. I spend the last hour meandering through garden pathways, down to the river and along the ponds. What's really nice is that the trails are either dirt or brick which makes it easy to walk quietly.

I see one small alligator, though the day is too cold for them. I wander high ground and low and take many photos of those massive trees. It would be wonderful to go back sometime. They say the best time to visit is the end of March when all the azaleas are in bloom. I stop in the museum gift store, buy post cards and three books. Two were on the Middletons and their slaves and the third is about plantation mistresses. Hmmm, think a little reading might be in order for tonight.

DAY 12, FRIDAY, FEBRUARY 1

No, No, No, NOOOO!!!!

It's February. I'm chilled and turned on the heat. I plan to stay here another day as Friday is usually one of my work days, but there is nothing in either of my folders. I've not done Drayton Hall or Cypress Gardens, yet I'm feeling the need to move on. Savannah will be coming up and Gail is waiting for me in Jensen Beach, Fla. I will be disappointed in myself if I don't do Cypress Gardens and if I put it off until I'm headed back north, I'm not sure I will do it. I've already by-passed things saying I'll do them on the return and even when I said that, I knew there'd be the possibility that I wouldn't. I know me.

That's a pattern in my journeys whether it's small ones, like visiting a favorite hiking place or a bigger adventure like heading off to new places. The going out is always with excitement balanced with introspection. My footsteps are light. I take my time and revel in what I discover. I'm relaxed and very much in the moment trying to see everything and taking lots of photographs or writing poetry. I love every minute and my heart is filled with joy. My demeanor changes when it's time to return home. At that point, I want to be home that instant and my footsteps are hurried and heavier. Things I thought I'd photograph or explore on the way back are ignored. It's almost as if I get some kind of message in my head and a homing beacon drives me. Home becomes my focus and I can't wait to get there.

Yesterday marked a day that was the longest I've ever been away from home in one stint. I am a little homesick. I miss my kitty and it still brings tears to my eyes when I think of her being all alone and missing me. Yes, Karen goes over every day to make sure she has plenty of food and water and take care of the necessary. (I don't miss the cold and the snow.)

I am afraid that when I start feeling that I want to be home NOW, I won't take the time to visit the places I put off on the way down. I also know that I'll regret it. There's already a part of me that wants to be home now. Being on the road can be tiring. Having to go somewhere every day when much of my time is normally spent at home alone goes against what I've built for myself. Living out of a suitcase and constantly dragging luggage around is a nuisance.

Life is quieter back home; living on a simple side road away from town surrounded with mountains and meadows. Here with the six-lane divided highways and constant drone of traffic and feeling crowded with buildings and people, I am feeling . . . overwhelmed. Ach, maybe I'm just missing family and friends.

But, I am not ready to call it quits! There is so much more to see and I am excited about that. Maybe this means that I cannot sit in this hotel room today; that I have to get out and do something. I could start some of my ITR work. I could write my neighbor column and get the community calendar set up. Then when the items I have to edit and new entries start coming in, I'll just have to contend with those.

Maybe I'm just feeling a little down this morning. Maybe I'm disappointed because there were two days of 70 degrees and now it's back down to the 50s. There was a time when I could have done half a dozen stops in one day and now, I can only handle one. What do I have to complain about? This is the most incredible opportunity I could hope for! I have GOT to do and see as much as I can.

After my shower, I plug the SD card from the camera into the laptop then check the InterTown Record folders while the photos upload. There are a few items and I do the editing, put together the community calendar and write my weekly column. A couple hours later, I remember the SD card. I pull it out, plug it back into the camera and erase the images. Back to the laptop, I open the Camera Upload folder in Dropbox to see how yesterday's pictures came out. No new photos. Oh, no! Where did my photos go? I click on the dropbox icon in the lower right corner and it says something about downloading 266 files and there are 19 hours left. What's with that?

I grab the SD card back out of the camera, hoping against hope. No hope. My heart drops. The computer says the card is empty. No, no, no! I am crushed. All those photos I had taken at Middleton Place are gone. I am devastated and totally discouraged. I feel sick to my stomach. I can't fathom losing all those pictures. I try looking up help in Dropbox, but that just brings up simple FAQs. I try looking in other folders and places on the computer. What happened to the pictures? I can't believe they're just gone.

By this time, another hour or so has passed and it is 12:30. I need to get out of the hotel room for awhile. I need to get away from wallowing in self-pity over my error with the pictures. The day is beautiful and sunny with the temperature only 58 degrees. I'm off.

Visit to Drayton Hall

Drayton Hall, Magnolia Gardens, and Middleton Place are all within six miles of each other. These plantations consisted of thousands of acres in their heyday. Drayton Hall appears to be the smallest and the brochure doesn't tout beautiful gardens like the other two, which is why I saved it for last. The front of the main houses faces the river because the Ashley River was the major transportation route. The carriage road approached the rear. The homes also had front and back porticos. During the humid summer months, the big doors could be left open for cross breezes.

As I return to the area, I consider running up to Middleton Place to see if they'd just let me grab a couple photos to replace the ones I lost, but it's getting late in the day. I turn in the gate at Drayton Hall, a long fairly straight driveway. At the ticket booth, the guy tells me that the man who started this place was the third son of the Drayton's who owned Magnolia. Knowing that he'd never inherit that estate, he bought this place consisting of 350 acres. By the time of his death, he had acquired 70,000 acres throughout South Carolina.

The ticket man also says that the white people often giving these tours downplay the treatment of the slaves. Slaves were treated poorly and often beaten. I realize he's probably right. The last two places, although they mentioned some hardship and inequality didn't go into the actual treatment of the slaves. Focus is more on the good that the slaves did, how they preserved their cultures, and all the knowledge they brought with them.

I suppose it would be hard to maintain these historical places and keep people visiting if the tours were about how poorly the wealthy planters treated their slaves. It was said that some people refuse to visit places that once had slaves. I can understand why they feel that way, but it is part of history and it's important to educate people about these times. The truth should be told, so hopefully, it could never happen again.

For families, it must be hard to think that their ancestors owned people and treated slaves horribly. It must also be difficult to work for a place that condoned that type of behavior. However, these places are preserving history and teaching visitors what plantation life was like. It's an eye-opening experience to find out that some of the men who are heroes in our history books had this darker side. Many of the planters were instrumental in America's fight for freedom.

There's a lot that the history books don't teach. For me, visiting these places and hearing the stories has put southern life in a different light. The humidity, diseases, the entire culture that has been drilled into the southerners' heads since infancy, the roles people were forced into and the consequences for those who deviated from society, and the extremes that the wealthy went through to maintain the hierarchies are beyond my comprehension. This is a culture so different from what I know. It's intriguing, fascinating, sometimes horrifying, and I want to know more.

I continue on to the parking lot and enter the museum to get a map. The lady tells me where to wait for the tour that would be starting in 40 minutes. She smiles, she's polite, but she doesn't make me feel welcome, nor does she tell me to look around the store. This is a gift shop. Shouldn't I be invited to look around? I feel snubbed. I walk out thinking there isn't any way I am going back to buy any souvenirs.

The incident makes me think about "southern hospitality." For the most part, people are polite, friendly, full of ma'ams and thank-yous, but there can be coolness to that warmth. It's almost like they're playing a role and if they're asked to step out of that scripted part, they go all, "Whayalll, Ah don't knos abou dat." Like when I asked the lady at the South Carolina Visitor Center a question about North Carolina, just up the road and when I asked the girl behind the desk if she knew where there was a camera shop. They pull the Sargent Shultz act, "I know nothiiinng."

Maybe it's my mood. Maybe I'm projecting the mood from my stupidity with the photos taken yesterday. I wander over to the Big House (what the main houses were called on plantations) to the spot where I was told to wait. The path is very hard and has shells imbedded in it. This is tabby, a mixture of oyster shells, limestone, sand, and water used in walkways and walls. I settle on a wooden bench and write in my little book. The air is chilly and I keep getting up to move into the sun. I take pictures of a few of the huge oak trees. My first impressions of this place are disappointing after seeing the gorgeous landscapes of the last two places. There aren't any fancy gardens here, just huge lawns.

Nearby is a small brick building. Outside is a sign stating Privy 1791. It's empty inside except for pictures on the walls of plantation life. On the back wall is a depiction of what this privy looked like years ago. It shows a long plank running the length of the wall with seven holes. I can't understand this. Did seven people use the outhouse at the same time? Was there no privacy? Did men and women come here at the same time? I try to picture it . . . and can't. There are no explanations and I leave the building feeling very confused about this issue.

Two couples and the tour guide show up. The draw to this house is that it has been preserved as it was back in the mid 1700s. That means no plumbing, no electricity, etc. The only updates were roof and window replacements and whatever else is needed to keep the building standing. Hurricanes have been the most damaging and the giant earthquake in 1886 took down the two flankers. There are no remnants of those buildings, just a huge manicured lawn. There are no flower gardens like the other two places. The back lawn (back because the big houses faced the river not the road) has a three-tiered circular mound in the middle. After the beautiful places of the last couple of days, this one is highly disappointing.

A Little Drayton Hall History

This property and Magnolia were owned by members of the same family. John Drayton, as third son would not inherit what is now Magnolia, so he purchased the land where Drayton Hall now sits. In the mid 1700s, with money earned in the cattle business, Drayton began turning the property into a rice plantation.

Building rice fields was an enormous endeavor and could not have been done without slaves. Banks of dirt had to be built to keep out salt water. Ditches were dug and gates constructed to control the flow of fresh water. For 50 acres of field, there might be 5,000 feet of ditches. Between planting and harvesting, the fields would be flooded and drained. They had to be weeded and birds kept away. Harvested rice had to be flailed, hulled, and polished before being sold.

During the Revolutionary War, slaves were often taken by the armies. Drayton Hall was used as a military base for the British. Corn became the major crop as it was less labor intensive than rice. After the Civil War, there were few slaves left to work the fields. Some stayed because they had nowhere else to go. Plantation life was over and properties fell into ruin. The remaining rice fields were destroyed by Hurricane Hugo in 1989.

From the late 1800s to early 1900s, phosphate was mined on the property with a strip mine about 1,000 feet from the house. It was ground and used for fertilizer.

Today, the lure to Drayton Hall is it's the oldest unrestored plantation house open to the public. The house, Palladian Georgian in design, is amazing with its limestone steps leading up to a portico. To help in the preservation, tourists are instructed to use one set of stairs and the next tour group the other to save on the wear and tear of using the same ones all the time.

Intricate Details

Inside, most of the walls have only ever received one coat of paint. Every window has a window seat. The walls are made out of cypress and are absolutely gorgeous. Cypress is a good insect deterrent. Porcelain knobs on the walls once held paintings. The wood carvings of the trim and the hand plastered ceilings are stunning. This is the first place I am allowed to take interior photos.

After the tour, I head out on the marsh walk. It's quiet and peaceful, some views, but not much. Trees with Spanish moss overhang the walkways. Yellowed saw grass rises tall from the wetlands. The grounds away from the main house are overgrown and former rice fields filled in. Depressions in the earth and ditches can be seen. I hurry along. It's getting late. I don't see any birds and find this place not so exciting. Hmph, it's probably just me.

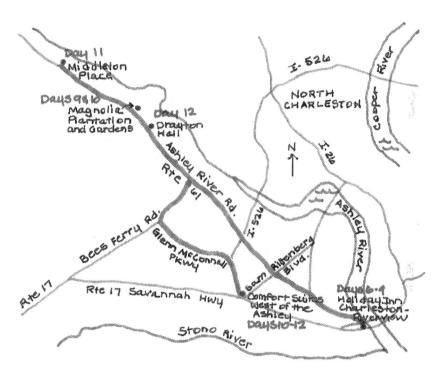

Around the Charleston Area

DAY 13, SATURDAY, FEBRUARY 2

Cypress Gardens, S.C.

I wake up about 2 a.m. to use the bathroom and get back into bed hoping the awful headache will go away. Half an hour later, I'm up at the pain reliever bottle. I toss and turn until 4:30. I'm still debating visiting Cypress Gardens before leaving Charleston. That would mean going north and to the west of the city. Part of me just wants to head further south now. There's time to think about it. Maybe it will depend how much work I have to do this morning. I check my folders, nothing in them. Perhaps it's time to get cleaned up, dressed and packed.

By 8:30 a.m. I've made the decision to go to Cypress Gardens. The day is clear and sunny without a cloud in the sky. The temperature is supposed to reach 60 degrees, but only 53 when I leave the hotel and soon after I get on the road, the gauge drops to 43 degrees. I take Rte. 526 north. Uh, oh, there's a big sign saying, "Incident Ahead, Get Off at Next Exit." Vehicles line up for miles and we inch along. Luckily the off ramp has an on ramp directly across the other road so we are all able to get right back on the highway. Then, for me, it's Rte. 26N to Rte. 52. Sometimes I drive for so long that I wonder if I am still on the correct road before I see a confirming sign.

I reach the site around 10 a.m. The temperature has risen a whole degree. I put on sweater and coat, pay the entry fee along with a ticket for the guided boat ride. There are three miles of walking paths and 80 acres of open swamp. With a little time before the scheduled departure, I wander. A man and woman who come in behind me are birders. We chat about the birds we've seen. They invite me along as one of the workers offered to show them some of the bird sites. I tag along and we go over to the butterfly house where there is a painted bunting. He's beautiful, but up in a dark corner near the trunk of a tree. Not a spot to get a good picture. I do photograph a wood duck, two other birds, and a couple of butterflies.

When we get out to the swamp, the first thing I notice is that the water is like a slick black mirror which catches reflections in brilliant detail. The blue of the sky, nearly straight tall trees, and surroundings are just slightly wavy images on the smooth surface. I lean over a little bridge mesmerized by the black water. If I stare into the dark depths long enough will something profound happen?

Kathy's voice penetrates my reverie. She has spotted a pair of young eagles. She says it's unusual to see them this far inland as their main food source is along open waters. Hopefully my photos will come out.

It nears time for my boat ride and I head back towards the dock. I am Margie's only passenger. The boat is flat bottomed and sits low in the water. For me, it's quite a step down from the platform and takes a couple seconds to maneuver the walking stick to help me balance and lower myself into the boat. The seat is only a couple inches from the floor. My knees immediately begin to ache as I stretch them out in front of me. I haven't sat on anything this low in a long time.

Into the Boat

Margie takes a seat behind me and pushes away from the dock. We move across the water without a sound as she dips her paddle in the black water. There are many trees throughout the swamp and she carefully maneuvers the boat around them, through pond lily fields, and past tall clumps of saw grass. The cypress trees grow gray and tall out of the black mirrored water. I am intrigued by the clumps of vegetation growing out of the base at the water's surface. I ask if the waters are still like this all the time and she replies unless it's real windy. She explains that the needles from the cypress have a high content of tannin and the tannin turns the mud black. The waters are actually very clear. She says that a good part of this land was drained, dug deeper and refilled. The cypresses were planted by the owner.

I get mixed up on the actual time line. A lot of the land here was chartered in the late 1600s and most of the plantations built in the 1700s and then there was the Revolutionary War, the War of 1812, the Civil War, the Great Earthquake, and lots of hurricanes. In 1989, Hurricane Hugo whipped through and did so much damage that Cypress Gardens didn't re-open until 1993.

It is so peaceful out in the swamp. The boat quietly glides around the trees. The black mirrored surface of the water makes for wonderful reflections and I am fascinated by them. We talk about our homes. Margie is from Michigan and like many, wanted to get away from cold winters. I take many pictures as she tells me about the creatures of the swamp. She says, "It's too cold for alligators," and that I probably won't see one. She points to a couple areas where they come to sun themselves. We go around a couple more trees and I see something black at the edge of the water. It's an alligator! (What is even more exciting, when I later edit and crop the photo, I am delighted to find a little alligator by the back leg of the big one.)

Big One, Little One

Margie says to note its color. This one is dark black. She explains that alligators are usually gray, but that the tannin from the trees settling to the bottom of the ponds causes these alligators to darken. There are around 75 alligators here and they come and go. Alligators can travel over land and sometimes will move on to a new home and others will move in.

All too soon we head back. (Sighhhh.) I could stay out here all day. How nice it would be to just lie back in the warmth of the sun and let the boat drift quietly along. Margie points to two battered pillars still standing that had been erected for the movie "The Patriot" and says that the façade on the bridge is totally fake, made of Styrofoam for the movie. She adds that during filming, if any of them had been caught taking photographs, it would have been a $10,000 fine. Also filmed here were "Swamp Thing," scenes from "The Notebook," and more (I can't remember all titles she mentions.) She goes on to say that the swamp looks totally different today than when "Swamp Thing" was filmed years ago because of the damage done by Hurricane Hugo.

Back at the dock, I have a difficult time getting up out of the boat. First, I have to get my aching legs under me to stand. It's a long step up onto the platform for my short legs. The pain in my knees won't allow me to kneel on the pier. I struggle and with the help of one hand on a piling, the other grasping my walking stick, and a one-two-three oomph, I pull myself up.

Once on dry land I head off on one of the trails. The camellias are still blooming, though most have faded. Camellias are my new favorite flower. The azaleas are just starting to blossom. There is one that is a gorgeous shade of dark pink. This area must be really beautiful in the spring. I am told that late March is really the time to see flowers. The path wanders through flowering bushes, by tall cypress, over bridges giving views across the swamp. I see one more alligator, but not from a spot where I can get a photo. There are three different gazebos where weddings are often held and remnants of an old rice field. I finally see oak leaves on the ground that I recognize!

I make it back to the gift shop area. I check out the Reptile House and visit the exotic bird area. Kathy sees me and says that when I get to Florida, I should check out the Wild Life Refuge at Cape Canaveral. I promise I will. I purchase post cards on my way out. Guests are arriving for a wedding and I'm glad to get out before the crowd.

Leaving the Charleston Area

By 1:30 p.m. I'm on my way south. The temperature has risen to 49 degrees. It feels a lot warmer after all the walking. I make it back to Rte. 17S and begin the long drive towards Savannah. There are long desolate stretches broken by periodic towns and occasional river and marsh crossings. I'm in a hurry as always and don't want to take time to stop. My brain dulls with the driving and the hurry to get somewhere for the night. In this mindset, I miss a lot of scenery.

As the miles pass, I wonder again about the aloneness. I would not want to share a room with anybody as that would invade my privacy and distract me from my work. Maybe it's because I've lived alone for awhile. Maybe part of it is from an ex who used to complain I was a noisy sleeper, so that I am now self-conscious of annoying anyone else in the room. Maybe it's because of that same ex who used to insist on the television being on all the time and I like my quiet. With someone else in the room, I'd feel I'd have to talk or they would and that would break my concentration with writing or drawing.

I don't mind exploring places by myself, although having someone share the moments would be great. I like walking the solitary trails and I relish the silence, but for the sounds of nature. I don't mind being alone with my thoughts as wooded paths, garden trails, or boardwalks are trudged. When I am out in a beautiful, natural setting, I am totally one with the earth.

So, no, I am not lonely . . . except when I'm driving, I wish there was someone with whom to be excited about the sights. It would be great to have a passenger watch for signs and take a few notes. It would be nice to share, "What's that?" and, "Look over there!" I would love to have someone find words for the vegetation, trees, rivers, and mountain passes for which I have no names. It would be wonderful to have that person take in the things that I cannot because I have to pay attention to the road.

Maybe I should pick up hitchhikers. Okay, not a good idea. No one hitchhikes anymore and if they did, it wouldn't be smart to offer them a ride.

I make one stop at a place that sells ciders; peach, blueberry, blackberry and apple. I try the peach. It tastes like apple and is too sweet. I buy a cookie and whoopee pie. Rte.17S merges with Rte. 95. Now it's really boring. Should I try to make Savannah? I'm tired and having a hard time staying awake. I keep wiggling in my seat to keep myself awake. I shake my hands; first one, then the other. This is not good.

I pull off the highway when I see a Comfort Inn Suites sign. This is Ridgeland, S.C. The odometer reads 14,656.7. I've driven 1,490.6 miles since leaving home.

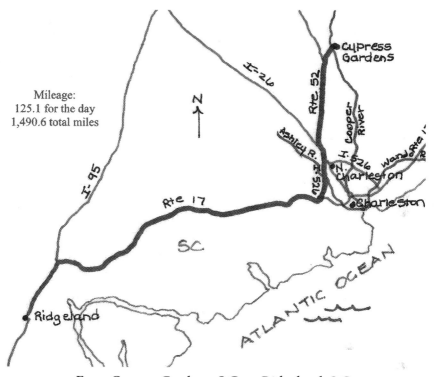

Mileage:
125.1 for the day
1,490.6 total miles

From Cypress Gardens, S.C. to Ridgeland, S.C.

I'm given Room 120 on the end near the soda machine and laundry facilities. It faces Rte. 95. I forgot to ask for a room away from the traffic. Check-out is noon which will give me time to do laundry tomorrow.

I settle in by 4:15 p.m. and I'm starving. I've only eaten that cookie and whoopee pie. Jasper's Porch Restaurant is across the parking lot and opens at 4:30 p.m. It's still a little early and when I sign on to the computer there is work for me in the *InterTown* folders. I send a quick message to Annette asking if I can do them in the morning, then I head over to the restaurant.

I order a glass of wine along with flank steak wrapped in bacon, baked potato, and mixed veggies. Ooh, sounds good. The restaurant sits near a pond and there's a walking trail. Perhaps I'll check that out in the morning. The wine goes down well and another is ordered. The trouble with eating alone is I tend to shovel the food in my mouth. Not a good way to eat. The steak and potatoes are delicious, but the mixed vegetables taste like overcooked cauliflower and it's mushy. I order coconut cream pie for dessert, but I can't eat much as it's way too sweet. Still, I'm satisfied.

When I get the bill, I'm pleased to see that they have printed suggested tip prices for 15, 18, and 20%. That makes it easy. I trudge back across the parking lot to my room. There's a beautiful pool and I'm too tired to swim. I kill a bug running across the vanity. Uh, oh, that's not good. I hope there's no more. The sink is dirty from spilled coffee. Ugh. I crawl into bed about 9:30 p.m.

What day am I on? Oh, yeah . . .

DAY 14, SUNDAY, FEBRUARY 3

On through Georgia

I slept fairly well last night though I'm right by Rte. 95. The off ramp has a funny surface and the vehicles passing over it sound like thunder. I've heard worse. I'm up at my usual time and finish the last of the work for the week and check over the room invoice. The price is $66.60 plus $4.66 for state tax and $3.33 for occupancy tax.

The tub creaks and groans as I shower. I worry it will fall through the floor. Wait a minute, I'm on the first floor and there is no basement. The toilet is the lowest I've ever sat on. I feel like I'm going to fall over backwards every time I sit down. Toweling off after my shower, I happen to look up at the vent on the wall. Ewww, I don't think it's ever been cleaned! That's gross and I will say something when I check out.

I head down to see what there is for breakfast and to get quarters for the washer and dryer. People are having biscuits and gravy and raving what a wonderful southern dish. I don't care for sausage, but decide to try some. It is good and I'll definitely look for this more often.

Back in the room, the internet is giving me all kinds of problems. A message keeps coming up about re-directing my pages. I never know what to do about things like that, so I click cancel. Now I can't post and will have to wait until I get to a new location tonight. At least I got my work and laundry done. By the time I'm ready to leave, I am feeling down in the dumps. Maybe it's the room, maybe it's that my clothes didn't totally dry, maybe it's the realization that I have been on the road for 14 days dragging luggage in and out of hotel rooms. Maybe I'm just feeling lonely and a little sorry for myself. Yeah, I guess I'm just having a bad case of homesickness. I miss my kitty. Then I think of that cold back there and I'm glad I'm down here. It's cold here, too, but I have all these new sights to distract me.

All of a sudden, I can't wait to get out of this hotel and hurry my things out to the truck. It's nice to be parked right near the door. It's clear, sunny, and 61 degrees. I stop at a BP station for gas and am pumping before I notice the price is $3.64. That doesn't make me feel any better especially seeing lesser prices at other stations. I get on I-95S and drive and drive; feeling sad and tired of being on the road. I miss our simple back roads. There are miles where there is little scenery, but for the scrub pines on both sides of the road. It's hard to look around going 75-80 mph. I cross the Savannah River into Georgia at 11:15 a.m. and shortly thereafter, pull in to the rest stop. The welcome lady says there are no plantations left in Georgia; the land has been turned into shopping centers and housing developments. I pick up a bunch of brochures and look them over. Nothing is appealing. After all the hype about Savannah, I'm just not interested. Guess I'm feeling too down in the dumps. I keep going on the interstate.

There's something mind numbing about the driving. If I concentrate on the highways and the traffic, I don't have to think. I don't think about the changes in my life. I don't wonder where my art is going nor do I have to think about marketing and selling my work. I don't think about selling the house or packing or fixing the yard. I don't have to miss my mother. My eyes tear. Stop that! I force myself not to think about her and I wipe away the tears and swallow the lump in my throat. I let the whine of the pavement put me in a trance.

The brain goes numb. The scenery changes, but I hardly notice, except to note areas of trees, sections of marsh and river, and passing through towns. In today's sadness, the sights are not exciting. I can't perceive it all. Part of me wants to be so busy seeing it all that I don't have to think about anything. Today, though, what I am seeing is meaningless. Even trying to explain this means nothing and part of me doesn't care.

Perhaps I need this numbness. Perhaps it's good to forget about normal life for awhile and let myself be free to do whatever I want in the moment. It makes sense. For awhile I can be free and not worry about the decisions that will need to be made this summer. For now, I can just be a traveler. And today, I'll accept that I am in this funk. Tomorrow will be better, I promise.

The miles go by and I focus on the freeway and vehicles around me. My world narrows to the road and seeing how far I'll get. I see brown historic signs for Jekyll Island. I remember brochures. Maybe I should take a break from the highway. It would be nice to see beach and the historical places there. That area sounds interesting. In my current mood, I can't make myself take the turn. Perhaps when I come back north, I'll spend time out there.

I continue south. I notice red buds on the trees. Back home we won't see that until April, if we're lucky. There's green on the trees and even more trees. I cross many rivers and creeks and every once in awhile, I get a quick look out over marsh fields. The Atlantic Ocean is out there to the left somewhere. At 1:30 p.m. I cross the St. Mary's River into Florida and stop at the visitors' center.

This place is huge and very busy. The walls are full of racks of brochures and paneled cubicles contain more. Each section is of various areas of Florida. I am in a state of "I don't know what to do." I'm leaning towards St. Augustine, but I'm not sure. I'm totally depressed and brain dead. I start talking to a lady behind the counter, but she's quickly distracted by someone asking more direct questions. I wander around feeling indecisive and out of place. I find brochures for the area around Port St. Lucie and Stuart which cover Jensen Beach where Gail is staying.

A man approaches and in a thick accented voice, asks where I'm headed. I saw him behind the counter earlier, so I know he works here, but I'm leery. He says he's the manager of the Comfort Suites in St. Augustine and he volunteers at the Welcome Center one day a week. He offers me a free upgrade to a room and I take him up on his offer. He makes the reservation and gives me directions.

Back on Rte. I-95S, I have about an hour's drive to St. Augustine. First I have to pass through Jacksonville. There's a 295E and a 295W. I have no idea if I should take either of those so I stay straight on I-95. The speed limit drops to 55. Jacksonville is HUGE! It's scary. Most of the way I feel I am driving over the city. I keep my eyes right on the traffic in front of me. My heart is pounding. There are bridges and cloverleaves and ramps, some above and some below. It seems they are going every which way and I feel I am in some kind of futuristic movie. My mind babbles at sights for which I have no words. Staying straight and true on 95, I get through the city and the speed limit again is 70 mph.

By the time I see Exit 318, my mind is numb again. I'm tired. I take the ramp off the highway. Again, this hotel is close to I-95. The odometer reads 14,856.1; 1,690 miles from home and 199.4 miles driven today.

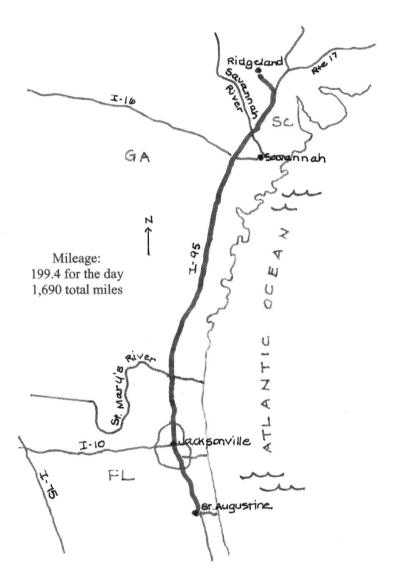

Ridgeland, S.C. to St. Augustine, Fla.

The lady at the desk is telling the people in front of me that there aren't any vacancies on the first floor. The manager had registered me for the first floor. I tell the woman that it doesn't matter to me which floor as long as it is quiet and I can still have that upgrade. She gratefully assigns me a third floor, room 309, and lets the couple have my reserved room. Everyone is happy.

There is only an outside pool here. She gives me a funny look when I ask if it's open. I don't say anything more with other people around. What, just because it's a little chilly people don't swim here? This is Florida, after all.

Bringing my luggage in on the trolley, my CD player falls off and now won't work. The room makes up for it. This is the best I've had yet. There's lots of space. Maybe I'll find a place to buy a new CD player. St. Augustine has lots and lots of shopping places. Maybe a little shopping will cheer me up . . . not that I like to shop, but buying myself a present would be okay.

After I settle in, I head across the driveway to a little diner. I ask for a white zinfandel and the kid brings me white wine which I find dry. I have a burger and fries. Back in my room, I check in on the laptop to let everyone know where I am. Afterwards, I chill out and look through the brochures. There are different tours I can take through the city. This is another place where a shuttle will take me downtown. Decisions, decisions; I need to rest.

DAY 15, MONDAY, FEBRUARY 4

St. Augustine, Part 1

The early morning is spent importing, editing, and posting photos to Facebook before taking a break to run down to the breakfast room about 8:30 to have half a biscuit and gravy. I tell the front desk that I'll stay another day or two and ask about train tours. There is shuttle service from the hotel to the location and I will not have to drive. Yes!

Back in my room, I struggle to get more photos posted. Some will upload quickly while others have to be canceled before trying again and again. Finally, I get enough done to give everyone a glimpse of the places visited. Now, it's time to get outside for awhile. The front desk is called to arrange for the shuttle. I decide to bring my backpack in case I find something to buy. I'm at the truck dumping unneeded things out of the backpack when the driver shows up. He says a sweater isn't needed as it's going to warm up. I should have taken the sweater.

This van is taller than the one in Charleston and it's not easy getting in with my short legs, bad knees and the height of the step. The running board is a narrow strip of aluminum and I'm leery about putting weight on it. I have to turn my foot sideways which makes it a little difficult getting the other foot by that one along with the backpack, walking stick, and camera. There's a couple in the seat behind the driver which means squeezing into the far back. It's a tight fit, but I manage and settle in for the ride.

The Red Train Tours, owned by Ripley's Believe It or Not, are small train-shaped engines which pull two open-air cars each with six bench seats. There are 22 stops throughout the city and ticket holders can get off at any stop, get back on, or stay on for the whole tour. Then it begins all over again with the drivers switching off. A train comes along every 20 minutes. Just be at one of the stops. I buy a three-day pass because everything can't be in one day. Many of the stops are shopping areas, restaurants, or churches. Other places are points of interest and historical sites. Some of these charge a fee to get in. Tickets can be bought with the train ticket for a discount, usually $1 off admission. For today, I'm going to do the city tour, look through some of the shops, and visit the pirates' museum.

I ride the train through one complete loop to get the feel of the city. What fun it is to be able to do this. One could ride around all day. This gives me a brief history and a better idea of which places to visit. The Spanish architecture is amazing; style, colors, and materials. I thought Charleston, S.C. had history. St. Augustine is even more fascinating. What is remembered of American History pretty much started with the Pilgrims and Plymouth Rock although I do vaguely recall reading about Jamestown and Roanoke. Some of the old walls that protected original settlement are still standing.

Old City Gates

Ponce de Leon actually landed in what is now St. Augustine in 1513. He used to be on Columbus' crew and later petitioned for his own fleet. From then, the Spanish took over rule from the natives. The city of St. Augustine was actually established in 1565 making it the oldest continually occupied city in the country. The French had a go at trying to take the city, but were defeated and there were years of issues with the British.

Someone said, "How would our history have been written if told from the Spanish point of view or the Native American point of view?" Now, that's food for thought. History, as I know it, was told more from a wealthy white man's English point of view with a New England influence. Charleston, though different from New England, also had British origins (after the Native Americans.) Down here in Florida, the Spanish influence makes it totally different.

After completing one loop of the entire tour, a new driver takes over. They each have their own spin on the stories, so even though the basic history is the same, there is a different take and other points are made. Part way through the second time around, I get off in a shopping district. I'd seen a sign for Birkenstocks and could use a new pair. Nothing appeals to me. I buy some post cards in a little shop nearby then step into a place called the Silver Feather to buy earrings. This is my kind of place with dream catchers, stones, jewelry, and books. My eyes light on some feathers; a turquoise strand and another of purple. Oh, dragonfly earrings in turquoise and purple. How can I resist? The store clerk suggests hooking the feather strands to my walking stick. What a great idea as the other feathers are looking a bit tattered.

Around the corner of a counter, my mouth drops open. Against the back wall are seven racks of Native American flutes. Oh, my. Different styles, makers, wood, sizes, and keys. I have to try some of them and pick out four small ones and play a little on each one. Hmmm, I don't know. Then my eyes light on one that has a different mouth piece. It's by a different maker, smaller, made of bamboo (which I don't have) and in the key of E. I raise it to my lips and play a rift. Ohhhh, I have to have this and a few minutes later, I walk out with a bigger bag and lighter pocket.

I stroll around other shops, but don't feel like buying anything else. I find the Pirate & Treasure Museum and run into more transplants from Connecticut and Michigan. I guess I'm not the only one wanting to get out of the cold. Many people come to stay. The woman behind the counter and I chat about New England until others came in. The museum is set up to resemble a pirate ship. There are hundreds of artifacts that have been discovered throughout the years. Video and audio places are available and I hop from stool to stool to hear tales of the 10 most famous pirates. (I never knew Sir Francis Drake was considered a pirate . . . guess he was to the Spanish.) Hovering over display cases, I am intrigued by the tools; the different sextants, telescopes, and such and even more impressed with the tools for cartography. I always wondered how they made maps. This museum also has one of the only true remaining pirate chests and an original Jolly Roger flag.

After a burger and fries at an outdoor café, I make my way back to a trolley stop in that area. There are many huge buildings with gorgeous architecture built by Henry Flagler. Flagler was already quite wealthy when he teamed up with John D. Rockefeller and together they founded Standard Oil Company (now Exxon.) Flagler's plan for St. Augustine was to turn it into southern version of Newport, R.I., catering to the rich for their winter get-aways.

Another point of interest about St. Augustine is that this is where the Emancipation Proclamation was read for the first time in Florida. Dr. Martin Luther King and Dr. Robert Hayling led the last campaigns here that brought about the passage of the Civil Rights Act. It's said that King had to stay in a different house every night he was in the city for safety reasons.

The day hadn't gotten warmer and I am freezing on the way back. Thankfully, it's warm inside the van for the ride to the hotel. Billy, the driver, talks about other places to visit. The Alligator Farm has an amazing bird sanctuary and none are in cages. I should be able to get some fabulous photographs. There's also the Fountain of Youth and yes, people are allowed to drink from it. The Castillo de San Marcos will be interesting as it has seen wars, invasions, pirate attacks and has never been taken in battle and it's said that the St. Augustine Lighthouse has spectacular. I will not, however, climb the 219 steps to the top. If I did, I'd probably have to be hauled away on a stretcher.

The next two days should be great fun.

DAY 16, TUESDAY, FEB. 5

St. Augustine Part 2

Sixteen days on the road, I can't believe I've been gone this long. I'm having a great time except for missing "real" conversations with friends. Yes, I've called family and I have good e-mail and Facebook conversations, but I do miss physically seeing the people back home. I keep running into people here in the south who used to live in the north. I think I've talked to more people from Michigan than anywhere else. Connecticut comes in second.

Still, this trip is immensely enjoyable. The history is so fascinating. I don't know what I was thinking, but it is very different than New Hampshire (at least to me.) It just goes to show that each area is unique. And Florida, being originally a Spanish colony, is even more different with the eyes noticing right off the architecture of the buildings.

The plantations that I visited on the way down had European influences, especially as the original owners wanted to set themselves up like British aristocracy, wealthy gentlemen farmers with a touch of Roman and Greek in some of the fancier architecture. Some of the gardens not only had an English flair, but French, too. In St. Augustine, the Spanish influence is in the style, type of materials, and colors. The Villa Zorayda Museum is even more outstanding as every window in the building is a different; size, shape, angle and color painted bright reds, yellows, and blues. Supposedly, the building was styled after the Alhambra in Granada, Spain.

A couple days ago, I mentioned tabby. Here construction was done with coquina; any kind of shell mixed with limestone and water. When hardened, it's like concrete. The city of St. Augustine, at one time, was walled and could only be accessed through a gate. Those walls, built of coquina, also had a defensive aspect. Anyone trying to climb the walls could get severely cut.

Today the plan is to get a photo of Magnolia Avenue, said to be one of the most picturesque streets. It's no longer lined with magnolias, but with majestic live oaks covered in Spanish moss. Live oak is an extremely hard wood and was used to build many ships including the USS Constitution. Also, the natural curves in some of the trees were excellent for the ribs of the old ships. The churches are amazing, too. Churches usually are beautiful.

I import and edit the photos I took yesterday. There are more than I thought. I upload 18 to Facebook and now I'm ready for today's adventure.

Alligator Farm

There are decisions to make of what to do today; the Fountain of Youth, San Sebastian Winery, St. Augustine Lighthouse, the Old Jail, Castillo de San Marcos, and the Ponce de Leon Hotel (which is now Flagler College.) Many buildings in the city were constructed by Henry Flagler. Flagler had churches and hotels built and he even established the railroad here.

The shuttle van arrives to pick me up about 10:30 a.m. This day I wear my sweater. I have an easier time getting in this van. Red Train Stop #2 is the shuttle van's base. This sightseeing tour company is owned by Ripley's Believe It Or Not and the museum is just down the street. Strange atrocities are not appealing and I have no desire to go there even though it is one of the train's stops.

I buy a ticket for the Alligator Farm and decide not to do the lighthouse, both of which are over the Bridge of Lions on Anastasia Island. People have told me that, as a photographer, the views from the lighthouse are spectacular, but I can't see spending the money when there is no way I'm going to climb 219 steps to the top.

Stop #4 is the home for the shuttle to the Alligator Farm and lighthouse. The driver is out on a run, so I chat with Melissa, the woman minding the shop. She is from Michigan. I haven't had many real conversations with anyone on this trip and she and I hit it off. She says she got tired of the cold winters and after a first visit here, fell in love with the area and made the move permanent. We talk about the north versus south and kids now-a-days.

The driver returns and again, I'm the only passenger. We cross the Bridge of Lions to Anastasia Island and a short time later, he drops me off. The Alligator Farm is entered through the gift shop and a turn-style. On the other side is a series of wide, elevated boardwalks meandering back and forth. There's a sturdy chest-high wooden fence to keep visitors on the boardwalk and alligators off. An unpleasant odor hangs in the air or maybe I should just call it unusual. It's probably due to all these different species. A toucan is behind heavy screening, which is not conducive to good photographs.

Next are white crocodiles and alligators. I take a photo of the Albino American Alligator and one of a bunch of tiny baby alligators. I shudder to think of many little creatures crawling all over me. Then there are LOTS of alligators of all different sizes. I keep hearing a noise like a huge rumbling snore and it takes awhile to figure out from where it's coming. It's the alligators! There are so many. It's creepy. I'm glad I'm up high.

White Alligator

Bright blue catches my eye. Birds! Blue, red, and green macaws and parrots all posing to be photographed. We don't have these in New Hampshire. Then there is an ugly, strange looking, long legged bird with a big bulbous growth hanging on his throat. It reminds me of a turkey's wattle, only this is bluish and like a half-inflated balloon. It almost looks like it's diseased. A sign says Marabou Stork, which can stand up to five feet tall and have an eight and a half foot wingspan.

One of my favorites is the pair of West African Crowned Cranes. They neck and preen each other. How sweet. Also in this enclosure are white buzzards and other vultures. Evidently, they have just been fed because they are all squabbling over stuff on the ground – I don't care to know what that is. The driver on the way over had told me that if there are too many baby birds in a nest, a parent will "accidently" cause the weakest to fall to the ground where it is quickly devoured by an alligator.

I continue along the boardwalk, which is high above the alligator enclosure. Some are quiet while others are thrashing around in the water. Some are HUGE! There are so many alligators that anyone falling in during their hungry period wouldn't stand a chance. Good thing the fences are high and strong. I take photos of Galapagos turtles and more alligators. Overhead in the trees are zip lines and a ropes course. This is truly an adventure park.

The boardwalk meanders towards the rookery. I am more interested in the birds than the alligators. White birds are in a huge tree in the distance straight ahead and high in a tree off to the right is a nest with something pink and yellow in it and I wonder how they got pink and yellow ribbons up there. I extend the lens of the camera. Is that alive? It moved. Oh, my, gosh, are there young this time of year? I can't really tell at this distance and snap a photo anyway figuring it can be cropped later for a closer view.

Baby Roseate Spoonbill

Higher up in that tree is an ibis and many photos are taken of them and yellow-crowned night herons trying to catch some in flight. The herons seem to be mostly sleeping.

Not all of the birds in the trees ahead are white, some are pink. There's one wading in the water and it has a funny looking beak. Oh, it's roseate spoonbill. What a strange bird. Its colors are a beautiful shade of pink. The gray bill is long and narrow until the end where it flares out in the "spoon." It looks so heavy; almost as if the bird would fall forward. I catch something flying. It's one of the spoonbills and it flies to that nest that I'd seen earlier. It must be a baby there!

I learn more about wading birds: tri-colored heron has a grayish bill, yellow legs and white belly with thin neck stripe; green herons have dark bills, yellow-orange legs, and deep chestnut necks; and the reddish egret has a pinkish black-tipped bill and bluish legs.

There's a museum depicting stories of some of the largest alligators and crocodiles known. Snakes are curled up sleeping this time of day. I photograph the Komodo dragon and outside is a tri-colored squirrel. I have had enough alligators and look for more birds as I continue the loop around the swamp. Before leaving, I stop for a burger and fries at the snack shack. The root beer tastes like it was made with the swamp water. I go outside to wait for the shuttle.

On to my next adventure . . . it's only noon, plenty of time.

Castillo de San Marcos

My intent on leaving the Alligator Farm is to go to Flagler College. Imagine seeing the first hotel that had electricity (five years before the White House) and to see $40,000 worth of Tiffany windows. We get back to Stop #4 and I sit on the bench awaiting the next train.

Suddenly, I change my mind. I want to buy a pair of red earrings and head back to the Silver Feather where I'd made the purchases yesterday. It takes a bit of hemming and hawing, but the choice is a pair of coral disks with silver design. They go well with the wolf pendant that I wear. At another shop, I purchase a pair of sunglasses. By this time, the day has warmed considerably and the sweater comes off. Heading towards the fort, I take an old side alley. The bricks are horribly uneven and I carefully watch my footing. It would be easy to twist an ankle. The last building at the corner of the main thoroughfare is a coffee shop. There are patio tables outside in a little courtyard and a woman is sitting near the sidewalk with a huge piece of pie. I have to ask.

Key lime, that's a key lime pie? Oh, I have to have a piece. This gives me the opportunity to sit, take the backpack off, and tie the sweater around it. That pie is delicious. One problem with traveling alone is that with no one to talk to, I eat too fast. There's so much to do and see and after returning the plate and fork, I head across the main street to Castillo de San Marcos.

From the street, it just looks like a low cement wall on a hill. I walk up the incline to the ticket booth and pay my fee. From this height, it's beginning to look like a real castle. A drawbridge is crossed to the ravelin, a triangular fortification in the middle of the moat. Wow, who could tell it would look like this from the road! From this vantage point, walls are tall and an impressive structure can be seen. Turning a corner, I walk down a long ramp, cross a smaller drawbridge, and enter the interior of the fort through the sally port, the only entrance.

First is a dark, damp, cave-like room. It's like stepping back in time; as if the world on the outside is in another dimension. A shiver goes through me. Straight through is access to the inner courtyard under bright, sunny skies. Both entrances have a huge iron gates. On either side of the room are doorways leading to more dank rooms. I go to the right and enter a barracks room with short narrow beds. The Spaniards were not tall. Rough mattresses are on the wooden frames and it does not look comfortable. There is barely room between each cot for a man to stand. The ceiling is curved with one window near the top. What a depressing place to live.

Sleeping Quarters

109

I go out in the courtyard. It's a huge area and I picture Spanish soldiers drilling and practicing on the grounds. To the right is a double wide staircase leading up to the terreplein (platform around the top.) I want to look around down here first. I follow the walkway to the left and enter a room. Visitors can access most of these rooms that ring the perimeter and many have storyboards and photos telling about the history and building of the fort.

The Spanish began building the fort in 1672 and it took 23 years to complete. It is the oldest masonry star structure in the U.S. with four corner bastions. The walls are 10-feet thick at the bottom and four at the top and it's all made out of coquina, as were most buildings around the area.

Coquina is a mixture of shells, limestone, water and mortar. The city had been burned a few times and people found that coquina doesn't burn like wood. Plus, cannon balls tended to sink into the material rather than shatter it. The walls were originally painted white with red corners (the colors of Spain.) One of the stories goes that the Spaniards, after the British shot cannonballs during the day at the fort, would rappel down the walls after dark and repaint the walls where the cannonballs hit. When daylight came, it would look to the British as if their cannonballs had no effect.

The British held the fort for some time, so there are British influences among the Spanish. I still can't get over all this history. It boggles the mind that these structures have lasted for hundreds of years and even though some areas have been rebuilt or added to, parts of the original buildings are still visible.

A small school group of kids with a couple of adults enter the fort. The parents or chaperones sit on benches outside while most the kids are running around screaming in the rooms to hear the echoes. These antics are disruptive and annoying. They are also running up and down the steps and I'm afraid they are going to bump into someone and knock them down – I don't want it to be me. Why are kids allowed to run through historic places creating havoc? These places are not playgrounds.

I slowly make my way up the top stopping a couple times to rest and take pictures of the coquina walls and steps. Imagine some of this dating back to the late 1600s. To be able to touch these walls is amazing. On top, the views overlooking the Bay of Matanzas are stunning with the bright blue of the sky, the streaks of white clouds, and the turquoise of the water. (Matanzas is Spanish for slaughter and the name given to the bay when the

Spanish executed a shipwrecked crew of French when they refused to convert to Catholicism.) I explore this upper level taking many photos and looking inside the bastions, but run out of energy before making it around to the other side. I haltingly make my way back down the steps. It's 2:30 and I'm ready for hotel time.

Bastion with a View

Great Meal and Conversation

I get back to the hotel around 3:30 p.m. and settle in to import and edit pictures taken earlier before heading to dinner a little after 4 p.m. The woman at the desk recommends Giovanni's, an Italian restaurant. I want to get my truck washed, but there's no one at the car wash and a meter thing asks for a security code. Maybe that means I have to go to the gas station and pay. I choose to back away, but not before I see a van pull away from the gas pumps and hit a cement post denting the passenger side of his van. A couple of guys sitting in a tow truck nearby laugh like crazy.

This is one of those deals where I have to pull out of the hotel going the opposite way and get over to the left to get into the U-turn lane further down. Both times I pull out in front of someone I never see coming. Gosh, this traffic is moving fast. I'm sorry, guys!

Giovanni's is at the end of a little strip mall. I am hesitant, but enter. "Are you joining me tonight?" a nice young man asks. "Are you joining me?" I ask in return. There aren't any other customers, so after bringing me a salad, glass of white zinfandel, and water, he stays and chats. Normally, that makes me self-conscious, but it's good to have someone with whom to talk. He makes recommendations on dinner and I take his advice and order one of the house specials. It's a chicken Alfredo that also has tomatoes and bacon in the sauce on top of linguini. Oh, my, gosh, it's good! I can't eat it all and have leftovers to heat up later.

It feels so good to have someone take the time to talk to me although I am worried because he is supposed to be working. Sloan Blevins grew up on a farm in Tennessee, but is living here now and going to school in Jacksonville to be a welder. He already has a job lined up when he graduates. He and his fiancée are expecting their first child. We have a great time talking about vacations, families, and farming. We commiserate on coming from a very small rural town and ending up in a city. I talk about New Hampshire and he talks about Tennessee. He says his grandmother is an artist. Too bad more young people aren't like Sloan. Growing up on a big farm, he knows what it is to work hard. He also has a lot of courage to come to a school far from home and to an area so different from what he is used to. I wish him and his fiancée the best of luck.

It's getting late now and my poor tired brain and body need rest.

DAY 17, WEDNESDAY, FEBRUARY 6

St. Augustine Pt. 3

I am back at the writing by 5 a.m. and post some of the edited pictures from the Alligator Farm. The morning is overcast and gray. I'm wearing red today so I can wear my new earrings. Last night I couldn't watch my favorite television show, "NCIS." Comcast was down for some reason. I didn't bother calling the front desk. I was able to watch stations like the Food Network and I've been enjoying "Storage Wars" on the History channel and "Pawn Shop" on A&E. I miss my DVR.

Commercials are horrible and having to sit through them is torture. Most are disgusting. Personally, I'd rather have the old beer commercials back. At least they were entertaining. This crap about drugs, "Ask your doctor about . . ." is crazy. Hello, wake up! Talk about becoming a drug dependent society. Oh, wait a minute; these are okay because they're approved by the FDA. Ha, what a joke.

It's raining. What will this do for today? There's an umbrella in the truck, but to carry something else is not something I care to do. It's hard enough to rely on the walking stick and still be able to manipulate the camera. The weather says it's just going to be cloudy. I am ready for the day's adventure and off to see what I will see.

Old Hotels

The rain let up, but it is still cool and misty. The van picks me up at 9:45 a.m. and at the train station, I am given a new sticker and a rain poncho which will only be worn if it rains harder. I'm too late for the Flagler College tour which began at 10 a.m. The architecture is so intriguing that I can at least take photos around the outside and get off train at the stop across the street.

Pictures are first taken of Villa Zorayda, which is America's first poured concrete structure. Franklin W. Smith had it constructed in 1883 to resemble one wing of the Alhambra Castle in Spain. It's now a museum. What's fascinating about this building is that no two doors or windows are alike. All the trim is painted in bright colors of red and yellow with occasional touches of vivid blue.

No Two Portals Alike

Flagler College was built as the Ponce de Leon Hotel and made with poured concrete. Henry Flagler hired Thomas Edison to install electricity and Louis Tiffany to decorate. It is said that servants were hired to turn switches off and on because people were afraid of the new technology. The architecture with its Spanish Renaissance style is amazing. I am so intrigued that I dare to venture inside the first gate. This entranceway is a wide hallway around the perimeter with brick and red tile. There are red-tiled carvings of lions on the columns. I can't resist going through the next iron gate into the inner courtyard. I love the concrete walls with the red tiles adorning windows, doors, balconies and roof. What would it be like to go to school here?

Taking more courage, I climb the steps and go through the front doors into the lobby to photograph the rotunda. It's huge. I can't even begin to describe the elaborate scrollwork and carvings all in gold and browns. There are towers, balconies and rows of columns with hallways on each level leading off from this center area. An elaborate stairway leads to the arched balconies which look down on the lobby. I don't even have the terminology to describe it.

Domed Rotunda

Outside, I walk down the block, around the corner, and halfway down that block to photograph the dining room where there is the largest collection of Tiffany glass in the world. Unfortunately, there's a lot of construction going on and I can only get a partial photo of the outside of the round room.

Flagler's second hotel, also poured concrete, was built directly across the street from the main entrance of his first. Four stories tall and constructed in 1889, it was originally called Alcazar in which were Turkish baths, early motion picture shows, bowling alleys, and the largest indoor swimming pool at the time. It's now the Lightner Museum and St. Augustine City Hall.

I bypass the museum and go through to the huge courtyard which is surrounded on all four sides by the building. There's a lush garden with flowers and palm trees around a long garden pool with fountains and a footbridge crossing in the middle. Exploring a long corridor with archways down its length, I take photos of angles and lamps. I want to find the pool which is so long, that the outside wall of the building was built with a bump-out curve to accommodate it. Today the pool area is a restaurant.

A small ante room has old photos of what the pool looked like in its heyday. The pool itself was 120 feet by 50 feet, three feet deep on one end, 11 feet deep on the other, and open four floors up where the glass ceiling could be cranked open. Gentlemen usually hung out at the shallow end because then they could still smoke their cigars. Second and third floors rim the perimeter where anyone on those levels could look down on the pool. The second floor was for musicians and guests to relax and the third floor contained the ballroom.

I go farther in and find I am in the shallow end of the actual pool (there's no water now.) I could never have imagined what this would be like and I'm having a hard time taking it all in. It's not easy to describe. Today the areas directly under the second floor balconies are small antique shops. I have no idea what they were back in the day. There is a set of stairs leading to the second floor at each corner of the pool. I decide to explore the upper floor before lunch. As in other places, the architecture is opulent. Well, it had to be, as Flagler's intent was to entice wealthy northerners to winter here. I walk around the balcony checking out the alcoves and rooms. One of the long sides has an entrance to the upper level of the museum. I decide not strain my knees with a third floor climb.

Once a Pool

I descend to the pool floor and head towards the café. It's odd to walk into an empty pool, feel the slant and knowing this was once held water that would have been over my head. I sit at a little bistro table. There is dampness in the air and I feel a little closed in. I order a classic club sandwich with baked chicken, bacon, cheese, lettuce and tomato, mayonnaise with a side of red potato salad. A glass of white zinfandel adds a nice touch.

A man at the next table begins conducting business on his cell phone. How annoying. There goes my peaceful lunch. People always seem to talk louder on the phone. Just before I leave, another man sits at the piano and begins to play. Now, that's nice. Too bad I'm on my way out. I'm not sure what I want to do. I walk back towards the center of town and find the area of the shops again and eventually make my way over to the Castillo de San Marcos. I consider exploring the rest of the fort that I didn't see yesterday, but I'm tired and catch the train back.

The Fountain of Youth

With the ride, I rest up. It's still early, so I get off at the Fountain of Youth. Inside, the first things that catch my eye are the peacocks. What beautiful, vibrant colors. The long bridal-veil like tail seems to have a hundred eyes. Some are even all white. They're not afraid of people and pose and preen and chase each other. When I speak to them, some come up to me. Aww, guys, I don't have any food.

A boy chases the birds and his parents never say a word. Yes, kids need to run off energy, but there are appropriate times and places. These historical sites are not the place for children to be wild and disrespectful to other visitors and cruel to the animals and birds.

The actual Fountain of Youth spring still runs and is housed in a small building. People are allowed a small cup of the water. It tastes like it came from the Alligator Farm and smells like water from the faucet in the hotel. If I remember correctly, one of the guides this week said something about the water here containing sulfur. That would explain the odd smell that seems to be in quite a few places.

A different door is exited and I continue exploring the park following its pathways. The peacocks and other birds are wandering around loose. This park has been undergoing archeological digging since 1934. There's a huge corroded cannon atop a mount made from coquina and an 800 pound clay pot over 300 years old which was once used by the Spaniards as a water cistern and would be buried half in the ground to keep the water cold.

I walk down to the edge of the estuary where a long boardwalk extends out to the river. This was where Ponce de Leon first landed.

A Long Pier

Juan Ponce de Leon arrived in 1513 and is noted for "discovering" the Fountain of Youth. Pedro Menendez de Aviles arrived in 1565 to begin Spanish occupancy. However, the area was already home to the Timucuan Indians and after a few years of hostilities, they came to terms and in 1572, St. Augustine became the first successful European settlement in the country.

It is a long boardwalk and I stop often to get photos of herons and cranes. I even take a few of the huge cross across the river at Mision Nombre de Dios, possibly the oldest mission in the United States.

The 208 foot Great Cross is constructed out of 200 steel panels and weighs 70 tons. It was a gift from the Catholic Church to commemorate the spot where St. Augustine got its beginnings. It's the tallest cross in North America and the second tallest in the world.

A long walk out means a long walk back down that straight boardwalk and by then I ache. I head over to an area where a lone woman is working on a clay pot. This area was set up to depict the life of the Timucuan Indians, who were here before the Spaniards. They were mostly wiped out from European diseases. The woman pulls over a bench and I sit and chat with her. She says the Indians were much taller than the Spanish.

After a rest, I do little more walking around then head out the front gate where I shoot photos of the street and the wall. I hop on the train when it comes back around. I'm done. I don't bother with the Old Jail. Bill brings me back to the hotel where I do my daily blog and call it an early night.

DAY 18, THURSDAY, FEBRUARY 7

One More Tour around the City

Big dilemma today; do I stay another night or do I head south? If I take one more ride around the city, I could stop at the Silver Feather and get Gail a pair of earrings. I should bring her a gift. She's patiently waiting, but eager for me to come. I'm looking forward to walking a beach and I am ready to be gone from this hotel. Next one, I must ask for a room on the end.

I spend two hours working like crazy to edit photos. I took 204 yesterday. Okay, I admit it, I get a little carried away, but most of this traveling is so exciting. I've definitely fallen behind in my editing. There will be a lot to do when I get home. Organized is something I am not and it bothers me. All the plans made before the trip are going awry. I'm not surprised. There are just not enough hours in the day . . . hours in which I have a lot of energy, that is. I know me and the one thing I do know for sure is that what I do seldom goes according to plan. It's good to be spontaneous and go with the moment. I like being able to change my mind in an instant.

Shower done, dressed, and directions to Gail's checked. I decide to forego laundry and leave St. Augustine. I had promised I'd come on Thursday and it is Thursday. Now it's time to pack up. Before leaving, though, I will do one more tour of the city. While I stack the luggage in the truck, the front desk calls the shuttle. I wait and wait. A different driver comes along saying the other is hung up in traffic because of downed power lines. It's a good thing Kathy and I spend time talking before leaving because I turn around before I get in her van and the door to my truck is wide open. How did I forget to close that! It would have been horrible to return to find my vehicle cleaned out.

Kathy and I have a good chat on the way to the Red Train Station. She had gone to the Picasso exhibit in town and talks about some of the pictures. I'd read a biography on him not too long ago. He was not a nice man. He treated everyone horribly and they worshipped him. Maybe they noticed his genius, but that doesn't excuse his actions. Personally, I find his work disturbing and wouldn't waste the $10 to see the show.

The lady at the ticket booth lets me ride for free as it was my fourth day. I hop off at Stop #4 head to the Silver Feather where I pick out a nice pair of dragonfly earrings for Gail. It will be nice to bring her a gift. She's always doing things for me. From there, it's a short walk over to the Castillo de San Marcos where I catch the train and then the shuttle to the hotel. I'm sad to be leaving St. Augustine. There is still so much more to see and more to learn, but it's time to move on.

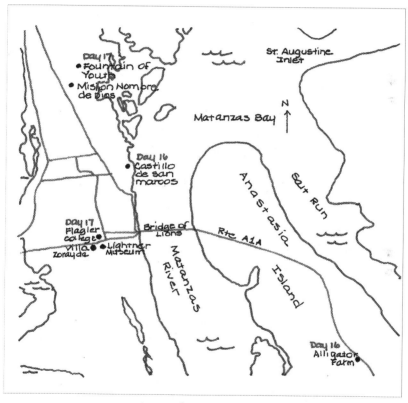

Around St. Augustine

On the Road Again

The sky is cloudy with the possibility of rain. At the Sunoco station at the end of the driveway, I fill up with gas (should have done that when I arrived as the prices went up) and I go through the car wash. A few minutes later, 11:40 a.m., I am on Rte. 95S. The temperature is 75 degrees. Gail said Jensen Beach is three and a half hours. I am in for a long drive.

At 1 p.m., I pull into a rest stop just south of Port Orange and gobble down two pieces of leftover pizza. The temperature has risen to 81 degrees. I don't need to be wearing the turtleneck I'd put on earlier. I should stretch and walk a bit, but I'm in a hurry to get to Gail's.

Speed limits fluctuate from 70 mph down to 60 mph in work areas. Miles and miles and miles of Rte. 95 are being worked on. The drive is tedious and there's nothing I find appealing. I begin to dislike Florida . . . a lot. This is weird and the antagonism about the state builds and the further south I get, the more ornery my mood and now I don't want to be here at all. If Gail wasn't waiting for me, I'd turn around and go back to St. Augustine.

Exit 126, Midway Road, is taken to head east to Rte. 1. Gail told me her place is a left off Rte. 1, so I stay in the left lane all the way through Port St. Lucie. Traffic light after traffic light and strip mall after strip mall all in heavy traffic; I can't even take my eyes from the road to look for a hotel. Rte. 1 is a six-lane divided north and south highway. Everything is straight and flat with side roads at right angles. Road signs warning which one is coming up at the next set of lights are in the meridian strip. I do not like this. Finally, I see the sign for Goldenrod Road, where I make one left, then another onto Cinnamon Circle. I have arrived.

Gail said to park next to her PT Cruiser, but I can't see it. I find her building, though. It's 3:30 p.m., 80 degrees and the odometer reads 15,062.9. I've driven 1,896.8 since leaving home. I'm surprised that as close to Rte. 1 as this place is, I can't really hear the traffic. The barrier fencing must work well.

Gail's dad says she's gone to do a little shopping. They have a nice little place for the winter and we sit in the living room making idle conversation. I haven't seen Clem since—I can't even remember—maybe 30 years. Gail returns and we are excited to see each other. This entire trip came to fruition because of her. I would have never dared to do this if she wasn't on this end of the trip and after over two weeks of not seeing any familiar faces, this greeting is even more special.

I change out of my turtleneck while she puts her things away. We head out to find a place for me to stay. She invited me to stay with them, but I like my privacy and I did not want to intrude. I take my sneakers off so I can walk barefoot in the cool green grass of their lawn. Ewww, it doesn't feel nice like the lush grass back home. This is rough, almost feels like plastic. Gail says it's turf.

The motels along Jensen Beach are booked, so we go out onto Rte. 1. She chides me for going through a yellow light saying that if the light turns red before I'm through, a picture is taken of the vehicle and I'll receive a ticket in the mail. Oh, great, something else to not like about this area.

I end up at the Hampton Inn in Stuart.

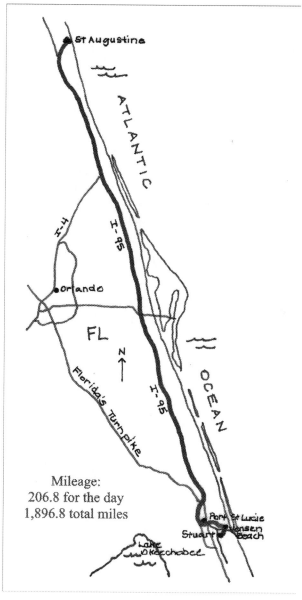

From St. Augustine to Stuart, Fla.

It's pricier than the places I've been staying in, but it's after 5 p.m. and I don't feel like looking any further. Gail helps me get my luggage to the room on the fourth floor then we go out to get dinner. She directs me to Tony Roma's in Jensen Beach. Thursday night is a happening night for the area. The restaurant is packed and the cacophony is deafening. Everything echoes and I feel very small and closed in. It's uncomfortable in here with the tables close together. I feel like I am sitting shoulder to shoulder with strangers and everyone else is in party mode. The meal is delicious, though. We both have fire-grilled chicken breasts topped with an apple-cranberry mixture, fire-grilled mixed vegetables, and I have rice.

I feel bad. Gail wants to hang out as there are vendors and street performers and happy happenings along the boulevard, but I've been on the road all day and I'm tired. I haven't checked in back home and people will be wondering as I always check in between 4 and 5 o'clock. Plus, this is the end of the week and I have work to do. I take her back to her place and find my way back to the Hampton Inn after dark where I have a great conversation with the lady at the desk while buying a couple bottles of water. She's originally from the northeast. By the time I settle in my room, it's after 7 p.m. I do a quick check in on Facebook to let everyone know I am okay.

Karen had messaged that she finally saw Freyja and kitty actually allowed a pat. Tears come to my eyes every time I think of my kitty missing me. I miss her so much, my furry little ball of joy. Then I remember all the cold and snowy weather back home and I'm glad I'm in the south. I cannot thank Karen enough for taking care of things while I'm away.

DAY 19, FRIDAY, FEBRUARY 8

Hampton Inn, Stuart, Fla.

This bed is the most comfortable I've slept in since being on the road. Again I forgot to ask to be put on the side away from the traffic. Not that it's bad from the fourth floor, but I still would prefer more quiet. Once dressed, I open the curtains and look down on the traffic. The sky is a heavy overcast.

I go down to breakfast and have a couple pieces of bacon. The one morning I thought biscuits and gravy might be good, there aren't any. Back in the room, I check in with a couple of people back home. There's a bad storm coming. It's looking scary. I start the weekly calendar and my column. By 11 a.m., I ready to get out of the room for awhile. There are only two items in my ITR To Edit folder right now. I'll tackle those when I get back. The skies have cleared and it's sunny. I'm out of here.

I am at Gail's by noon. We discuss bird sanctuaries and wildlife preserves and check possible places on the internet. She offers to do the driving and we take her father's van. I'm not sure my body and legs would squeeze down into her PT Cruiser. It's great having someone else drive; I get to look around and see some sights. We take Rte. 1, also known as SR 5, heading south. I take photos from inside the van as we go over the one-mile Roosevelt Bridge crossing the St. Lucie River. It doesn't take long to get to Hobe Sound National Wildlife Refuge. After looking inside the building at the reptiles in cages, we head out on a trail.

Hobe Sound Nature Center

This area is actually called the Sand Pine Scrub Trail and is part of an ancient high Atlantic Coastal Ridge. It was formed during the Ice Age by changing sea levels and wind-blown deposits. Much of the sand washed down from the Appalachians and Piedmont of the Carolinas and Georgia. When polar ice caps melted these areas became islands isolating animals which adapted over time.

125

Some of these plants and animals are not found anywhere else in the world. The only plants that survive are hardy and salt tolerant.

To my chagrin, the trail is all soft beach sand and narrow paths. Prickly bushes and vines make the path smaller in places. Gail scratches her leg on something with long thorns and my walking stick gets hung up in the semi-parasitic love vines, called so because of their reddish color. Hurricanes spread this parasitic plant which is over everything. Most of the trees are slash pines which are native to the southeast and are prone to lightning strikes in this area.

The temperatures are in the 80s and the sun beats down. Walking is difficult in the soft sand and the first part of the trail is uphill. When the walking stick doesn't catch in the vines, it sinks in the sand. My feet and knees hurt. I struggle and move slowly. One part of the trail is the highest point for miles around – which isn't all that high as Florida is flat and the views are just overlooking scrub brush. Every once in a while we get a glimpse of the river. Fires from lightning strikes and recent hurricanes have killed many of the scrub pines, the snags of which provide perching and nesting places for birds. Gail points out a nest in the distance saying she thinks there is a bird in it. I snap some photos, but until I edit them, I can't tell. The only creatures we see are a gopher turtle, a bunch of little lizards, and a couple of far off, high flying birds.

We reach a part in the trail where one way goes towards the river and the other back to the nature center. If we had taken that trail to the river to begin with, it might have been easier for me. It wasn't marked at the trail's beginning. Gail wondered when we started out if that was a short cut, but I elected to follow the trail signs. At this point, I'm done in by the difficult walking and too hot to follow the other trail so we head back to Jensen Beach for dinner at the Olive Garden. It is soooo good! The Olive Garden is one of my favorite places to eat. I am never disappointed.

At the hotel, we change into swimsuits and go down to the pool. The Pool Rules sign gives us a laugh. At other pools, besides some of the normal safety regulations, there were "No spitting in pool" and "No blowing your nose in the pool." This pool sign has another, "No one with diarrhea should use the pool." Oh, what pictures that conjures up in the mind, ha ha! I can see Gary Larsen having "The Far Side" fun with this. 'Course it would probably gross most people out.

The water is cool and once wet, the air cooler. I am self-conscious when a couple guys set up their laptops at a table nearby. They don't stay long. I do my pool exercises and after awhile, we get out to lie in the sun to dry and warm up. Afterwards, Gail gives me a great foot massage. I am hoping it will help the swelling. Unfortunately, it doesn't, but my feet do feel better.

DAY 20, SATURDAY, FEBRUARY 9

Morning Ramblings

Postings and photos from back home make me very glad that I'm in Florida. They are being hit with a major storm. My brain feels like a pinball machine as thoughts bounce around. What am I going to do about winters? For the most part, I don't mind living alone, but during storms, it's scary. It's spooky when the wind rattles the windows and threatens to rip the skylights out. I'm paranoid about losing power and dealing with snow. I am not physically able to shovel and snow blow anymore, which means I need to pay to have those jobs done. It's costly.

One purpose of this trip is to help me clear my head and figure out what I want to do with the rest of my life . . . or at least with the next couple years. Northern winters no longer excite me. I used to love them with the beautiful pristine snow creating gorgeous landscapes. Great for a photographer, but I'm tired of the freezing cold and having to bundle up in layers of clothes to go out. I don't want to do it anymore. What would it be like to split my time between north and south? I'm a northern woman, but now that I am south for part of this winter, I realize how enjoyable it is to be out of that area. Yes, it's still cold in places, but there's a difference. I have to figure out how to make this happen every year.

That means selling the house and getting a smaller place. The house is too big and fills up with clutter. The yard is too much to maintain and costs a fortune to pay someone else. The house deserves someone who would take care of it and the gardens. Could something be worked out where I could spend part of the year in the south? It would be wonderful if I could take kitty with me. The thought of selling is terrifying. I am a basket case when dealing with real estate and legalities. My brain goes on overload and I short circuit, snap, and freak out. Nobody wants to be around me in these cases. I am not a calm, reasonable person when dealing with these kinds of things.

My sons would like me get an over-55 condo and I'd be agreeable to that if I could find one where there would be quiet and I could have bird feeders. I love where I live and love my job with the paper, so I prefer to stay in the area. It would be nice to be in a place where I wouldn't have to worry about yard maintenance.

Oh, I think too much! It's time to shut off these thoughts and buckle down to work. I have my ITR work to finish up for the week and there are photos to post and more to import, edit and post. Gail is waiting for me to free up time so we can go do something. Right now, it's time to put a load of clothes in the washer.

A Strange Waitress

It's unfair to leave Gail hanging all day waiting for my call. I should have checked my other file earlier to know I had a lot to do. Listings for the month of March are coming in and there are others. More organizations are recognizing the benefits of the free community calendar listings for non-profits. Gail says she has some errands to run and will meet me here about 2:30. I have one more list of March entries to do when she arrives, but that can wait as the deadline is Saturday.

We choose the Cracker Barrel for a meal. Gail offers to drive my vehicle and I take her up on it. That gives me a chance to look around more. So many stores and nothing appeals to me. At the restaurant, the waitress comes right over and stands there waiting. We haven't even opened our menus. "Oh, do you need a few minutes?" she asks. Well, yeah.

The special is grilled chicken over rice. Sounds good and Gail opts for that, but I've had chicken the last few days and I'm ready for a steak. It's good. The waitress comes over three times while we are eating to ask if everything is okay. Gail finally requests a To-Go box and the woman disappears. A few minutes later she returns to see if we want dessert. She did not bring the To-Go box and Gail re-asks for one. We decide to split a warm Coca-Cola chocolate cake with fudge frosting and a scoop of vanilla ice cream. The waitress returns with our dessert and no To-Go box. This time, I ask for it.

The cake is absolutely deeelicious! I'm not a chocolate fan, but I could easily become addicted. The waitress returns to see if we want anything else.

"A To-Go box?" we say together.

"Oh, yeah," she mumbles and hurries off. She comes back yet again without the box. Gail again asks and finally gets the box. Then as we are getting up to leave, the woman comes rushing up, introduces herself and asks for our names saying she'll see us soon. She will? What a strange experience.

Our original plan was to go back to the hotel and take a swim, but Gail suggests taking a ride to the beach. I have no problem with that. Oooh, I get to cross another big bridge, the Jensen Causeway which spans the Indian River. I am ecstatic that I can take pictures in the moving vehicle. Why didn't I know this on the way down?

Gail talks about her youngest brother, Lyle, who lived among the homeless under the bridge. He passed away last year, which was one of the reasons Gail and her dad wanted to winter in this area. During their time of grief, they are getting to know a few of the homeless people living here. Gail's dad is spending more time with some of these people and learning about the life his son experienced. The stories are intriguing and heartbreaking. My heart goes out to these souls. Most are so trapped in their addictions they can't do anything else, and yet, they manage to build a community for themselves sometimes even looking out for one another.

At the beach, we find a parking space and get out. Birkenstocks are not good for walking in sand. Oooh, to go barefoot feels so good! Ahhh. I limp up the dune and get my first view of the Atlantic Ocean in Florida. Nearer to shore, the water is turquoise in color and further out is the darker blue green like New Hampshire waters. The waves are rough, crashing onto an eroded beach. From the top of the dune, there is a short drop off like someone cut it with a knife and the beach itself is a steep slope. Gail says that just the other day, there was a lot more sand. I take photos, but I'm not too impressed.

Closer to the water is a father with his three children. What a beautiful family. We guess the two little girls are twins. I don't normally take photos of people without permission, but I take a couple of shots with the girls' backs to the camera. They are so adorable playing at the water's edge. I'll never use the photo because I didn't dare ask.

Gail turns north out of the parking area to show me a huge house. It's on the Oceanside and gorgeous with that Spanish-influenced architecture that I've fallen in love with. I'd love to see the inside. We turn around and head south. I am hoping to find a smaller hotel. A lot of places look like hotels, but they are probably all condos as there are no signs. Crossing the city line into Stuart, we go over the Stuart Causeway, two big bridges spanning the Indian and St. Lucie Rivers on our way out to Rte. 1. How nice to be able to look around and not have to concentrate on the traffic.

Back at the Hampton Inn, we decide it's too chilly to swim. In discussing what to do tomorrow, we are at a bit of an impasse. Originally, I had wanted to go further south to the Keys and Everglades. Gail is adamant about not going near Miami. My grandfather used to live in St. Petersburg and I wanted to see that area and possibly visit Sanibel Island, but I am disliking Florida so much that I don't want to spend the extra time here. There's no real reason for these feelings. There's just something about Florida.

I show Gail a brochure of a nearby butterfly farm. We agree and she heads off for the night. I settle in to do my usual routine. I feel a little guilty because she wanted to go somewhere, but I am just not for doing much after 4 p.m. Before signing off the computer, I peruse websites for other area hotels as this one is a little pricey. There are two down the street that are under $100 a night, but they only have a two-star rating and while most of the comments are good, some are not. I'll decide in the morning if I want to chance a less-than place.

DAY 21, SUNDAY, FEBRUARY 10

Staying Another Day

After "sleeping on it," I decide not to change hotels. The time it will take to pack up and get everything out to the truck is precious work time. I'm falling behind on the blogging and posting pictures. This will give me the day to make up my mind if I want to go across the state. I've taken so much time in a few places and there are only nine days left of this 30-day trip. As much as I hate to think about it, I need to start thinking about heading back north. Especially as there are a couple places in Charleston to visit. That will mean a two-day stop. It doesn't look like I'll have time to do Savannah.

But do I? Do I really need to think about heading home right now? What do I have to go back to? Yes, I miss Freyja horribly. Yes, I miss Wednesday morning breakfast with Nan, Bob, Jane, and whoever else might show up. Other than that, what is there? Sitting alone in a lonely house? I don't miss the house. It doesn't feel like it's my home, not a forever home. It was just a place to live until my mother passed and now that she's gone, the house has too many memories of her. Yes, I love the view, but the house doesn't feel like me. It means nothing to me. One of my biggest wishes right now would be someone offering to buy it at a decent price. There's much packing to do and getting rid of stuff; work that is tedious and depressing. All I want to do is my art work and write.

Nothing on the breakfast bar appeals to me. I don't care that it comes with the price of the room. I'd rather go out to a real breakfast place. I limp out to the truck to get the charger for the cell phone. I might make a stab at another Verizon Store. Stupid thing, I can't even tell if it's charging.

I import 54 new photos and update my blog with the last couple of postings. I can't concentrate on editing because my mind is in such a quandary as to staying longer in Florida or heading back north. Will I regret not going to Sanibel Island? I have to admit, that outside of St. Augustine, Florida isn't "doing it" for me. Perhaps because it took so long to get here, this should be it for the year. If I'm lucky, I can come back for an extended stay next winter and see more Florida sites.

Oceanographic Center

After spending the morning catching up on work, I finally contact Gail and we decide to go to the Florida Oceanographic Coastal Center. First stop is at a Verizon Store to make another attempt at the phone. The guy doesn't take long to say the phone doesn't work right and to call Verizon for another phone. They could even overnight it to my hotel. (If I knew which hotel I was going to be at.)

We next pull into a gas station where the sign says $3.49. It's not until I am pumping that I notice the pump price is $3.73. Oh, no, in reading the fine print, there's a different price if paying in cash or using a credit card. I got caught trying to find a cheaper price when all the other stations were around $3.65. Yeah, it's more expensive down here.

Gail scrubs the windshield. Wow, that glass is filthy, but she soon has it spotless (with a little help from the Windex in the back) and we are on our way. The temperature is 78 degrees under sunny skies with fluffy clouds. We get to the Oceanographic Center on Hutchinson Island just after noon when it opens for the day. The island is a barrier reef between the Atlantic Ocean and Indian River Lagoon. It cost $10 each to get in and after getting our stickers we enter a room with aquariums. I am taken with the seahorses. What interesting creatures they are.

Outside, the first area is a sting ray petting pool. I ask the difference between a skate and a sting ray. (Unfortunately, I later couldn't remember what he said.) The guide shows us some cartilage of the barbs and mouth. The barbs detach once the ray stabs something with its tail. Gail asks about Steve Irwin's death from a sting ray barb and the man explains that unfortunate incident. Irwin had pulled out the barb and subsequently bled out. In a similar situation when a woman got stabbed, she didn't pull the barb out and at the hospital, they were able to do surgery to remove the barb and the woman lived. (The barbs on these rays have been removed so people can touch them.)

Sting Rays

We opt not to stay around for the feeding demonstration and head out towards the trails. The next enclosed pool area is huge. There are nurse sharks, more stingrays, tarpons and other fish. We take photos and move on to the nature trails. These are a hard-packed shell mixture with boardwalks over wet areas. I expected mangroves to be huge trees, but the majority of these are like small saplings. The leaves are similar to rhododendron leaves, but it's the root system of these trees that is amazing. The roots start higher up on the trunk than on other trees perhaps to be out of the water. They bow out and down almost reminding me of a crown with multiple root legs curving into the brackish water. Put many of these sapling-like trees together with this root system and there isn't anything of size that can get around in these swamps. It's very closed in.

In spots there are dry sections of land called hammocks on which there are dead trees and fallen palms. Some palm trunks stretch high in the air with no fronds on them at all. They look like tall posts. It's eerie. A few of the tops have other plants growing on them. These spots seen through bushes are brown, gray, and colorless. Other dead trees with their naked limbs stretch in creepy isolation as if green is afraid to be near them; as if something cut a swath through the green and left ugly brown, gray patches. I wonder if hurricanes caused this.

Gail is intrigued by some spiders. The manual focus on my camera does not work and when trying to photograph something in dim or shady light, the auto focus won't work, either. I can't get pictures.

The waters through the swampy areas are of various colors. Some are red, then there are streams of bright yellow, others are dark and clear, and there is a section where there is a whitish blue, oily yuck on the water. The colors, a sign reads, are due to the tannins from leaves and detritus that are rotting on the surface. It looks toxic and the thought of falling in one of these places . . . I can't imagine the diseases and infections. Then again, if these are natural phenomena for the area, maybe it's not bad. Very little of the water seems to be moving, it is stagnant, pools around the roots of the mangroves and most are full of mosquito fish. (Which aren't doing their job as Gail is bitten twice.)

Signs along the way explain the different vegetation and habitat of the mangrove swamps. We do a lot of reading and after awhile, we reach the Indian River, also known as the Intracoastal Waterway. The open scenery is refreshing. We look around a bit then continue along the trail which takes us back through the swamp. There isn't anything pretty about the swamp. It's too closed in for scenic views. Photos tend to be of specific leaves or plants. Still, it is interesting and a totally different landscape than I am used to. Gail reminds me it's because Florida is so flat.

Tri Colored Heron

We get back to the center in time for the turtle feeding. We watch for a couple minutes, but I'm not really interested. I am pleased that I was able to hike the entire trail. Yes, I am hot, my face is red and my left leg is dragging, but there is a breeze and enough shade so most of the walk wasn't in the full sun. I'm happy.

It is after 2 o'clock and I hadn't had any breakfast. We are both hungry and can't decide where to go. We end up at the Olive Garden again and enjoy another delicious meal. I eat too much salad (the waiter even gives me some to go.) Back at the hotel, we make plans for the morrow. Looks like it'll be a day trip to Lake Okeechobee.

I go over expenditures and work on my time line. I must have some receipts in the bag in the truck because I'm missing a few. I wanted to be so organized and keep careful records of everything. Oh, well, I should know me by now.

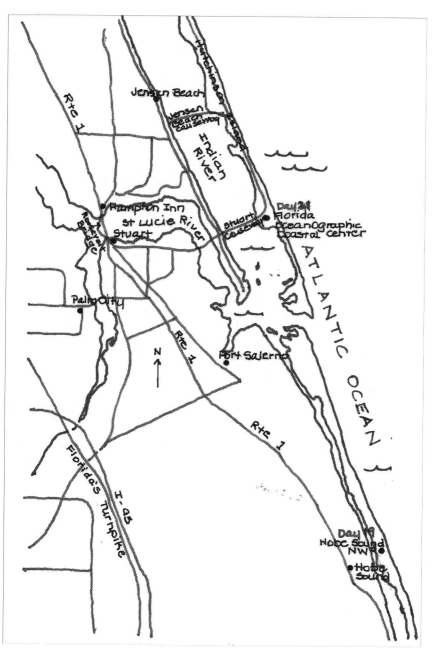

Around Stuart/Jensen Beach, Fla.

DAY 22, MONDAY, FEBRUARY 11

Admitting I Don't Like It Here

I ate too much salad last night and should know better. I was up a few times during the night and ended up taking a couple of aspirin around 2 a.m. for a horrible headache. Still, I'm up by 5 a.m., as usual. Hopefully, that lettuce will work out of me soon so my stomach will settle down.

I write about yesterday's adventure and import the photos. There are still days' worth to edit and post. Not sure when I will get to that. I should force myself to work later in the evening, but my brain goes into "du'uh" mode after 5 p.m. Typing slows and my spelling gets dyslexic. It's frustrating as thinking fogs over. It's like someone flips a switch and a "closed" sign is put over me.

After a lot of hemming and hawing about what to do, whether to head north or stay in Florida longer, I decide not to go across the state to Sanibel Island, nor go south to the Everglades or even further south to the Keys. Those areas had been on the agenda, but I just dislike Florida. However, Gail is enjoying my company and although I'm ready to head north to Savannah and then on to Charleston, I enjoy her company, too. I'm staying one more day here in Stuart. Today we plan a day trip around Lake Okeechobee. We Googled it yesterday and there are lots of walking trails. For me, it will be a nice, pleasant, quiet drive. Of course, it still could be a three-lane double highway around the lake.

It'll take two hours to get there. I'm definitely ready to get away from city-ness and out into country scenes. Yes, I got to see a little water yesterday and the day before, but I still feel I am in a city and it's too busy. Even if I don't see and hear the traffic, I feel closed in with too many buildings crowded in one area. It's almost like there's a constant hum against the energy field around my soul; like there's murmurings of conversation just beyond hearing and it's draining. The crowded highways, busy intersections, and miles of strip malls are depressing.

I discovered yesterday when we were looking for the Verizon Store that there are often whole rows of stores behind the rows along the Rte. 1. You have to pull into the parking areas or a side road to find what places are in the back as along the highway there are only a few signs. This is crazy! Sometimes signs are so small that they are unreadable until you're beside them and by then, you've gone past.

Okay, I'll admit this, and I'm sorry, Gail, but I don't like it here and the longer I stay, the more the feeling intensifies. Of course, she probably realizes that by now, even though I haven't come right out and said it. I feel bad because she has connection, history (she used to live in this area years ago,) and she's happy here. I want to like this area to please her. I am sorry. Okay, I got that off my chest. Now I can look forward to enjoying the day.

We always have a great time together and I'm excited about going over to Lake O.

Lake Okeechobee

Gail arrives and by 9:20, we are on the road with me driving; south on Rte. 1 in Stuart and right on Rte. 714. Within a short time, the three-lane divided highway narrows and becomes a simple two-lane road. Yes! Stores and businesses give way to open land. The sides of the roads are lined with palm and other vegetation, but in spaces, I can see farms and fenced in countryside. Miles can be seen if nothing is in the way and now with no buildings, I get a better understanding of the flatness of Florida.

It's nice to be able to pull off the road to take pictures. There are cattle ranches and horse ranches. To visit one would be awesome. I wish I dared knock on a door. Maybe they would love to show off their ranch and talk about what they do. As we continue west, trees spread their limbs over the road converging in a canopy and making sections feel like a tunnel. Even though I am driving, I haven't felt so relaxed in days. Ahhhh, this is enjoyable; driving through quiet countryside.

We pick up Rte. 710N to Rte. 70S then onto Rte 441/98S. At an intersection with the choice to go right or left, I cut into the right lane after being in the left because I see a brown sign indicating a scenic area. This is the top of the lake and from the road we can't see any water because of the tall dike. We drive up the lane, over the dike, and down into a parking area. The temperature is 80 degrees.

Lake Okeechobee is the biggest freshwater lake contained in one state in the lower 48, averaging only 9 feet deep. A rim canal around the perimeter is separated from the lake by a 100 foot wide dike. Atop the dike is the well-maintained, nearly

Sasha Wolfe

110 miles of the Lake Okeechobee Scenic Trail for walking, biking, rollerblading, horseback riding and bird watching. It is part of the 1,400 miles of the Florida National Scenic Trail.

Oh, wow! What beautiful blue water. A long pier stretches over the marsh area and for a distance over water. A covered pavilion is at the end with open sections extending right and left making the pier a huge T. We start out onto the boards. It's at least fifteen feet above the water. The shoreline to about thirty feet out is grasses and water vegetation. I photograph glossy ibis, egrets, green herons, a tri-colored heron, great blue heron, and various other birds.

Suddenly, the entire flock of terns and gulls that were in the parking lot fly off in a panic. The ibis and other birds hunker down in the weeds. My attention caught, I look to see what made them all take flight. Ohhh, what's that bird with a white head? Is it? I focus the lens of the camera. It IS! It's a bald eagle; there is the "bald" head and white on the tail. Wow! He flies to the top of one of the light poles giving me a better look. Too bad he's out of range to get a good photo.

Gail and I make our way to the top of the T taking pictures often. I even take photos of two lone pigeons hanging out with all the wading birds. It's beautiful and peaceful here. People are fishing from the pier and one smart old guy has a seated walker and a cooler. Ah, that's the way to do it. We take our time walking back to the truck. I am reluctant to leave this beautiful place.

Crossing back over the dike, I pay closer attention to the hiking/biking trail that runs the perimeter of the lake along the top of the dike. How brutal in the sun with no shade. Yet, there are people up there walking, jogging, and biking. Turning right onto Rte. 441/98S, we continue alongside the lake, but because of the dike, the lake can't be seen. Between the highway and dike are seedy looking mobile home parks after mobile home parks. Some advertise RV Camping. We come to another scenic view pull off and stop for more photos and discover a canal runs along the dike.

The next stop is at a small gas station/Subway to use the facilities. We get subs and snacks and at the next scenic pull off, find a spot of shade just big enough to fit the truck and we enjoy a picnic. After eating, we get out for more picturing taking. I find some big snail shells (big compared to what we find in New Hampshire.) Gail washes them out because one was full of ants. There are four, two for each of us.

My attention is next caught by rows and rows of palm trees on both sides of the road as we continue our journey. I'm intrigued by the pattern of the rows never realizing there was such a thing as palm tree farms.

Palm Tree Farm

The trailer parks give way to nice little homes on one side and ranches on the other. The highway back to the coast is coming along soon, but not before a huge bridge and another scenic pull off. This is Port Mayaca and a major access to the lake from the St. Lucie Canal which runs all the way to the St. Lucie River and empties into the ocean. We spend quite awhile at this place taking photos; not only of the scenery, but of birds, lines and angles.

Trail over the Lock

Back on the road, a big bridge crosses the canal. Rte. 76 back to the coast is a right hand turn which curves down, around and under the bridge and parallels the canal all the way to the St. Lucie River in Stuart. I pull over for some bridge shots before continuing on. A big flatbed passes by and the cargo catches my eye. Why does that look like clumps of grass? Gail says it's from turf farms and big squares are cut and loaded onto trucks to be delivered to other places. A turf farm; something else totally new to me and what an interesting place that would be to visit. As with the ranches, I wish I dared drive up to interview the owners. Turf, cattle and horse ranches would be great stories.

We leave the lake area heading east. Rte. 76 sees heavier truck traffic. I stop at a couple of abandoned places, but somehow, these buildings don't do it for me. There's a train trestle that is unique as it appears to be a drawbridge. Train tracks, like the roads in Florida, are straight for as far as the eye can see. Too soon we are back to busy Rte. 1 and all the stores and business. We arrive at the hotel about 3 p.m. The odometer reads 15,267.5. I've driven 2,101.4 total miles so far. It was a good day. This is the kind of peaceful sightseeing that is refreshing and inspiring.

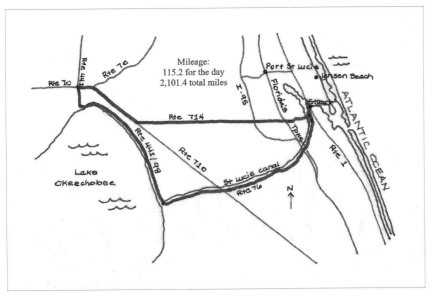

Along Lake Okeechobee

PART 2

RETURNING NORTH

Heading North across the Arthur Ravenel Jr. Bridge, Rte. 17

DAY 23, TUESDAY, FEBRUARY 12

Heading North

This morning I don't crawl out of bed until 20 minutes after five. Slept fairly well which is good. Packed up some things last night and soon I'll pack the rest. Gail is coming to say goodbye and help get everything out to the truck. She is such a wonderful person, good friend . . . more like a sister than friend. It's always good to see her. We enjoy ourselves even if it's just sitting around talking about when we were kids. I'm going to miss her.

Messages from home say they got more snow yesterday. I am not looking forward to going back. For now, I will just head north and take my time getting to cold country. I'm still unsure about Savannah and I don't know why. If Savannah is similar to St. Augustine and Charleston, I'm going to love it. Why am I hesitant? In going through some of the brochures last night there are quite a few things I missed in Charleston. That may be a three-day stopover at least. As this is day 23 of my 30-day journey, there's not many days left.

I don't know what today will bring besides starting the journey north. There's a possible visit the wildlife preserve on Cape Canaveral which was recommended by the woman at Cypress Gardens, S.C. A stop there would mean I won't make St. Augustine tonight. I'll see what the day brings. After all, this is about being spontaneous and I love the idea of going by how I feel in the moment.

I edit 31 photos from February 6. That's on top of what was edited last week. I'm not even editing every one. I'm starting to edit February 8 photos when Gail arrives. It's time to pack the laptop. We'll have some breakfast, say goodbyes, and I'll head north.

Oh, yes, it's a teary farewell.

Sasha Wolfe

Merritt Island National Wildlife Refuge

The morning is a balmy 75 degrees with a slight breeze and a bright and sunny sky. A couple little clouds break up the expanse of blue. I leave the Hampton Inn at 9:50 a.m. with half a tank of gas. Saying goodbye to Gail is tough and I pull onto Rte. 1 with tears clouding my eyes and after heading south to get in the other lane, I begin the return north. In Port St. Lucie, I turn left off Rte. 1 to go towards I-95. I am intrigued by the electric poles along the road. Throughout this journey I've been fascinated by the lines. I want to stop, but of course, in this area there is nowhere to be safely out of the way. If I pull onto a side street or into a parking lot, I will not have the angle that fascinates me. Anyway, getting in and out of traffic is not fun in this place.

I-95N is just as boring as coming south. An hour and a half goes by before I see the exit for the Merritt Island National Wildlife Reserve in Titusville. Oooh, another fantastic bridge! It's strange for a bridge this huge to have a speed limit of 30 mph, but it gives me the opportunity to look. Gorgeous views which might be why the speed limit is low as people are busy gawking. There are even sidewalks across the bridge with many people walking and enjoying the day. At 85 degrees, I'm not about to put myself in that much sun. At the foot of the bridge on Merritt Island are some pull-off areas for a boat ramp, picnic, and fishing areas. I'll stop on my way back (famous last words.)

The 140,000 acre wildlife reserve is at the north end of the island with coastal dunes, saltwater estuaries, marshes, scrub pine flats, hammocks, and more. To the south is the Kennedy Space Center and Cape Canaveral. Merritt Island is a 35-mile long barrier island located within the Atlantic Flyway, a major bird migration corridor and a key stop over for many birds. It's habitat for some of the highest number of endangered species known throughout the National Wildlife Refuge System with over 500 different species of wildlife and 1,000 types of plants.

I drive along a coastal marsh area with many ducks and some short squatty bushy trees growing in the water. The squatty trees might be mangroves. Again, I'll stop on the way back. I drive and drive. There are a few side roads and I wonder if they lead to viewing areas, but there are not any signs saying so. I keep on until I finally come to a visitors' center. A large tour bus pulls in behind me and while I'm parking, discharges a lot of kids. Oh, no, just what I need . . . NOT!

They are still getting off the bus and organized when I excuse myself by them. It's cool in the building and there are many displays. The ranger at the desk says there isn't any charge for the boardwalk, but there is a $5 fee for the scenic drive. I am getting the ticket when one of the others, hearing me mention that I'm from New Hampshire, says that one of their co-workers is from New Hampshire and points him out. I go over and find he lives just south of North Conway. He tells me he works down here in the winter.

I head out on the quarter-mile boardwalk trail. I love visiting these types of places and take photos of an osprey which I hope can be cropped to see better see the bird. Some people are excited over red-winged blackbirds and grackles giving me silent chuckles. They are some of my least favorite birds as they swarm the feeders in the summer and chase the smaller birds away. It doesn't take me long to do the loop. A lot of it is just various trees and bushes. The palmettos with their widespread fronds take up a lot of the views. Photos are taken of a baby alligator hiding in the weeds.

Resting Place

A left is taken out of the parking lot and I backtrack to get to the scenic road which turns out to be hard packed dirt and crushed shells; mostly a narrow one-car-wide, raised lane winding between marsh, mud flats, and little creek areas. This road surprisingly has quite a bit of traffic and there is very little room to pull over to take photos. I see interesting thistle growing along the sides of the road. I stop for photos of the landscape, vegetation, and birds hoping I'm over far enough for other vehicles to get by. There are a couple of serious birders out here with heavy duty tripods and huge telescopic lenses on their cameras.

At one stop, a reddish egret runs a few steps, flaps its wings, dip its beak into the water then turns quickly and runs in another direction to do the same thing. It's fascinating to watch and I take many photos. I especially want to capture the flapping of the wings and I'm not sure how the pictures will come out because of the distance.

Egret Dancing

The road winds on and on past creeks and through marsh. Where there aren't any trees, I can see miles across the flat expanse of open land with yellowed grasses and small creeks. And still the road meanders on. At midday, there aren't many birds. To be more specific, I see a lot of birds, but if this was early morning or just before dusk, there would probably be hundreds.

I stop at one place and hike out a trail that seems to stretch forever in a straight line. I see a viewing area ahead yet take time to photograph a couple of herons and ducks along the way. At the platform, all I see are crabs in the muck. There are three egrets in the far distance, but nothing I can capture with this lens. Still, it's a pretty area with more open water than I've been seeing. The trail continues on with a higher platform farther ahead. I walk about halfway, but I'm not seeing much. It's hot and the sun is beating down and as I'm not a sun person, I hesitate. People ahead of me who have reached that point aren't looking excited, so I turn back.

The drive goes on winding through the marshes, but it all begins to look the same. What birds I see are the species I've already photographed. After all the straight Florida roads, I should be happy to be on curves. At a fork in the road the map is checked. It looks like I need to go left. This section is horrible with deep holes and I have to drive even slower than the 15 mph limit. This can't be the right way out to the highway. Crap, it's a dead end. This is just a viewing area and at the moment, there's nothing to see. Arrgghh! There is barely enough room to turn around with water on three sides. Too close to the edge and it would not take much to end up in trouble.

It's getting on to 3 p.m. by the time I reach the main road. I haven't eaten since having a couple spoonfuls of home fries at 9:30 a.m. I'm ready for this to be over, but it continues. Ah, some stopped vehicles. They must be looking at something. I look to the right. About 50 feet away is a short tree in the middle of a creek with a flock of white ibis perched on the branches. It's surprising that those thin branches will hold such big birds. Well, yes, I stop, too, and take pictures.

Finally I come out to a highway and, according to the map, Rte. 3. The Manatee Viewing Area is to the left. The speed limit is 55 mph and tractor trailer trucks are whizzing along this road. I'm not sure where they are coming from and begin to wonder about the accuracy of the map they'd given me. (I later learn that the non-public part of the Kennedy Space Center is back that way.) At this point of the day, I don't really care about seeing any manatees. I'm tired and hungry. I follow a Florida car which had also come through the scenic route and we pull into a boat ramp area. This isn't the manatee area, but I do get some scenic photographs. Florida is still there taking his own photos when I leave.

After more miles, I cross a canal and just on the other side is the parking for the manatee viewing. I pull in and make my way to the area where many people are lined along railings. A ranger comes up and says there's a manatee at the other end and I realize this is the guy from New Hampshire that I'd spoken with earlier. He points through the brush and I can just make out the dark shape in the water. It's one of the big gentle creatures, but I can't see well enough to get a photo.

A big yacht passes under the bridge. One woman asks what impact the boats have on the manatees. The ranger replies there are about 75 manatees here and there isn't one that does not have scarring from propellers. Manatees are on the endangered species list. He also says that a couple years ago, a manatee was caught near Cape Cod when it got too cold for it. It's at the Aquarium now.

"There's one!" another woman shouts and I look where she's pointing and I'm able to get a shot of its snout poking out of the water. After awhile, I get tired of waiting for another to show. It's time to move on and find my way back to Rte. 1.

I pass an odd-looking white structure shaped like a round, many-faceted stone. A tractor-trailer passing by gave me a height reference. Three or four trucks could be stacked on top of each other and the building still might be a little taller. I have no idea what this could be and there are no signs.

End of the First Day North

I want to circle back to the bridge where I first crossed onto the island, so when I reach the major road, I turn south. I didn't realize how far north I'd come on the island and it's taking forever to get back to Titusville. I make my way back over the bridge where I pull into a parking lot and take pictures of the big bridge crossing the Intracoastal Waterway/Indian River.

By now, the gas tank is close to empty and it's 4 p.m. I drive towards Rte. 95, stopping for gas at a Sunoco station and by 4:45 p.m. I am in Port Orange settling down to dinner at a Golden Corral. It advertises buffet and WHAT a buffet! I pay for the dinner and a bottle of water and it only comes to $14.57. In the middle is a huge round area with any kind of salad fixings you could want. On one end of the room is a section of warm vegetables such as string beans, carrots, corn, rice and more; on the other side, different servings of potatoes, turkey and all the fixings for that. Around the corner I find the makings for tacos and Mexican-type fare. Then there's steak, Texas toast, rice pilaf, pasta dishes, and Oriental servings. I have steak, mashed potatoes, carrots and corn.

On the other side of the salad bar is the dessert bar with different pies, cakes, cobblers, puddings, and ice cream. This isn't naming everything that's there!

It is a good meal and I end with banana cream pie. I will definitely be looking for a Golden Corral for more meals, but for now, I need a room for the night. Country Inn and Suites is across the road and I have a coupon.

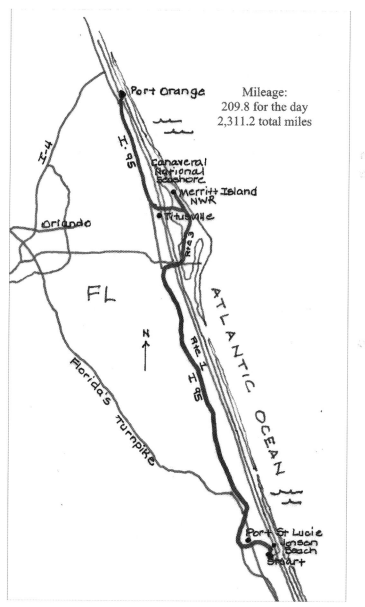

Mileage:
209.8 for the day
2,311.2 total miles

From Stuart to Port Orange, Fla.

Check-in is busy with people in line and people coming in. One woman wants the poor frazzled desk clerk to bring in her bags. The phone keeps ringing. I feel bad for the guy.

I take a trolley out to the truck and load it with things for the night. I can't wait to get to my room. The elevators are in a little side corridor on the left with a small table on the right. The trolley has to be turned to fit into the elevator and the space is narrow. Wouldn't you know, the elevator that opens is the one past the table so the trolley has to be squeezed by that then turned in a tight corner to get it on the elevator. Oops, I should have got on the elevator first then pulled the trolley in. Whew, I manage finally to get to the room.

Room 222 has a king-size bed. It's a nice room though it looks a little manly. Not that that matters. It's clean. The pictures on the walls don't seem to be the normal hotel reproduction kind of pictures that one can buy at Wal-Mart. These seem to be real art with giclees and nicely matted photographs. Very nice.

DAY 24, WEDNESDAY, FEB. 13

Into Georgia

Although the bed was comfortable, I was awake off and on during the night. Not a big deal. I am up at 4:30 a.m. checking messages and writing the blog. By the time that finished is finished, it's after 7. After a refreshing shower and cleaning up the room, I import 161 photos taken yesterday.

The morning is overcast, so I am surprised to step out of the hotel and feel the humidity at 77 degrees. The sun is trying to break through. I drive out of the parking lot at 9:50 a.m. leaving Port Orange without breakfast. As usual, nothing on the breakfast bar appealed to me. After an hour on the road, I'm hungry. I'd been seeing Waffle House restaurants all over the place and decide to try one out. I'd also been seeing signs for Florida Citrus and Souvenirs and both establishments are right next door to each other.

I order a classic waffle with strawberries and a side of bacon. I should have understood the menu better. It said strawberry and not "real" strawberries. It's a slimy syrup substance cooked in the batter which means the waffle is gooey. Yuck. I am too hungry to complain and it took too long to get this one. I don't want to wait for them to make me another. I eat almost all of it . . . barely choking it down.

The place is filthy and when I use the rest room, the floor is soaked and there is a big bucket in the sink. I'm not even going to guess what that means. I forget to ask what town this is so I could report that nobody should eat here. Although I say this, there are regular customers because the waitress calls them by name. Ugh, just get me out of here; this place is disgusting! How do places like this get licenses to operate? I would think the Board of Health would close them down.

I go next door to check out the souvenir place thinking that it might be nice to bring home some citrus to share. The grapefruit and oranges look beat up and inside the shop it's just one of those tourist-type places with what I consider junk. On top of the souvenir shot glasses and t-shirts are lots of shell jewelry. It doesn't even look it's made from real shells and feels like plastic. The place is dirty and rundown. Oh, I so want out of Florida.

Back on Rte. 95N, I run into rain. That slows most of the traffic, but not all. I stay in the middle lane and sometimes vehicles pass on both sides. Sometimes I pass, but always on the left. I worry about being caught speeding with all the camera traps and planes. It's scary to think that your picture is being taken all the time. I don't like it.

Driving through Jacksonville is an experience. For the most part, I-95 is straighter than straight; miles and miles of long, fairly boring road. In Jacksonville, the speed limit drops to 60 and the route winds above the city with long curves to the right, then curving to the left. There are highways and ramps looping above and below on amazingly tall concrete columns. As I said on the way down, it makes me feel I'm in a futuristic movie. I can't look around; my focus has to be on the traffic and making sure I stay in the correct lane. I would have loved to get pictures of all this.

The Georgia line is crossed at 12:30 p.m. I've driven a total of 2,438.8 miles and it is 80 degrees. I stop at the Welcome Center Rest Stop and ask about Savannah. It's a good thing I didn't get on Rte. 17 already. The lady here says if I did, I'd end up on the bridge crossing into South Carolina. She explains it a couple times. I'm confused. Oh, the bridge kind of goes OVER the city? Yes. She tells me of some options, gives me a map, and points to where coupons and other information are kept. I pull some from the racks and sit down to decide.

This is one of those times when I struggle. The Country Inn & Suites where I'd stayed at last night was very nice. There is one at exit 94 and another at exit 104. The welcome lady said I need to take Rte. 16 to get into the city and that's Exit 99. I leave the welcome center undecided and confused. When the time comes, I'll choose.

Oh, Savannah

There is better scenery now. Buds on trees show a pop of color; that light yellow green of new leaves when they first come out. There are also bushes with yellow flowers. Then there are trees with big red . . . buds? Leaves? They are a darker red than the little buds that we see in the north in the spring. I cross many rivers and creeks. Exit 5 jumps to something like Exit 26, Exit 37 and I feel better knowing that I'm not going to count exits one by one up to 94.

It is 2:30 by the time I reach Exit 94 and I decide to call it an early day. I check into the Country Inn & Suites with an indoor pool and a hot tub and this is the least expensive place I've stayed yet. I put my bags in Room 104 just down from the pool and walk across the way to Applebees. If I swim first, I will not want to get dressed again to get something to eat.

What do I want to drink? Hmm, I'm in for the night; why not get a big girl drink. Veronica is a great waitress helping me choose. I order peach sangria made with white zinfandel, Peachtree schnapps, pineapple juice, lemon and lime soda topped with fruit slices. It comes in a big heavy glass near to overflowing. I have to stand up to take the first few sips. Oh, my God! Is this good! I could roll right over. (Needless to say, I order a second before I finish my meal.)

For the meal, my usual Crispy Orange Chicken is ordered. They even pick out the mushrooms for me. I am a happy camper. I'm also pleased that Veronica is able to take the time to chat. She lived in New Hampshire for a few years and her sister still lives in Manchester. When I ask about sightseeing in Savannah, she calls to the bartender who is more familiar with the area. I thank Tammy for making a most awesome drink. She gives me tips on where to go and what to see. It's great talking to these two fabulous women. (I am the only customer at the moment.) I love it when the wait staff has the time to show some personal interest in their customers, plus it's great to find out something about them.

While I'm eating, the manager comes over and sits down to check on how things are going. We have a nice conversation. He says he lives in Charleston and tells me that there are walkways across the Ravenel Bridge. Hmmm, I would love to get photos from the bridge. Would I be up to walking it? He also suggests visiting Fort Moultrie, which is across from Fort Sumter. He prefers Charleston over Savannah.

I leave the restaurant with the usual leftovers and in great spirits. This place is awesome and I am thrilled with the conversations. They really made me feel welcome. This was the best meal time I've had the entire trip.

Back in my room and after setting up the laptop and checking in, I go for a swim. My cover-up isn't in the suitcase. I check the truck. Not there and then I remember I left it in the closet at the Hampton Inn in Stuart, Fla. Ohh, noooo! I am bummed! I never put things in the closet and I remember (now) hanging it up because it was damp after swimming. I'll never be able to get another like it. I bought it in the Caribbean years ago and it was also one of the only outfits I could put on when I hurt my back. I message Gail and ask if she could run over to the Hampton Inn and see if they have it. I still have my swim, sit in the hot tub a bit, and have another swim. That feels soooo good. Now I'm ready to relax and watch a little television.

I watch a couple of episodes of "Duck Dynasty." It's one of those reality shows where they follow the antics of a family. From what I understand, this family (I think they're in Louisiana) made it big on making duck decoys and duck calls. One son went off to college and was able to turn the family business into a huge success. After watching the two shows and seeing them trying to shoot beavers because the beavers built a dam which dried up their duck hunting pond, attempting to get honey from a beehive in a tree in the middle of the swamp, and hunting frogs in the dark murky swamp waters, I've seen enough.

On another channel I often watch, they were alligator hunting. No, thank-you. Oh, I miss my DVR. During commercials, I look through brochures and jot down some things that I missed mentioning in the blog. I finally give up and turn off the television. I can't hear the conversations well anyway and I don't want to crank the volume and disturb people in the next room. A guy in a big pick-up truck is sitting outside the window with his engine running. He's probably smoking as this is a non-smoking facility and it's raining. I crawl into bed with the sound of his truck vying with that of the air conditioner.

DAY 25, THURSDAY, FEBRUARY 14

To See the City

Valentine's Day and it means nothing to me; just a reminder that I'm alone. This is the one day a year that I really miss having a man in my life. Oh, well. It is what it is. It was a restless night as I was too warm even though I had the air conditioner at 68 degrees. After 24 nights I should know to ask for an upper floor and the side away from the highway. How long have I been saying that? That said, this is not a bad place. It's the biggest room I've stayed in so far and at the least amount of money. Two of us could do the Tai Chi form here. The skies are overcast, but it looks like it might clear.

At least seven rivers and creeks were crossed yesterday starting from the border of Florida and Georgia over the St. Mary's River. I try to list them using the map, but not all are in the atlas. This is when a part of me wishes for a traveling companion. There are things to photograph and notes to take; many things I miss and don't fully recall by the time I stop. Plus, stops can't be made every time I have these flashes of inspiration. For one thing, it's dangerous on the highways and bridges to randomly pull over and it would take forever to get from point A to point B. I can't cover everything. There's a huge amount of territory between here and New Hampshire. The landscape changes along the highways on both sides. There are palm trees, live oaks, and other vegetation. There are bare-limbed trees sprouting new green leaves or red buds. Then it changes to open marshlands along creeks or rivers where, if I dared take the time, I could see miles across the expanse.

I-95 seems to go over most towns. I get glimpses of the roads below which are often as straight as the interstate in both directions. Sometimes there are stores and businesses and in the bigger towns and cities, even those seem to go on and on for awhile. When I think about it, the interstate systems are phenomenal. The building of the major highways and bridges is mind boggling.

Today, I plan on entering the historic district of Savannah. There are a couple of trolley tours that have caught my interest and sound similar to the Red Train Tour in St. Augustine. I like the idea of having a number of stops where I can get off, wander around and be able to get back on later or at a different stop. I'll go to the visitor center to further my plans and buy tickets. A riverboat cruise might be interesting, too. There are Ghost Tours at night. Savannah was voted one of the most haunted cities in America, but being alone and not liking to be out after dark, I won't be doing this tour.

There's a Comfort Inn & Suites in the downtown area. Perhaps I'll book that for tonight and hopefully stay a couple of days. We'll see how it goes.

Savannah, Part 1

I am packed up to leave the Country Inn and Suites at Exit 94 by 9:45 a.m. It is 50 degrees; the temperature dropped from 80 degrees when I arrived. I go back to my room to put on a turtleneck and a sweater. (That poor sweater which I bought last month is looking so beat up now. The camera strap keeps catching and pulling threads.) I stop at an Exxon station, but don't get caught by the two different prices this time. Pay cash and the price is $3.59, use a credit card and it's $3.99 per gallon. I go inside and pay cash.

With it being so cold, (yeah, I know, 50 degrees isn't cold compared to what's going on back home) I consider by-passing Savannah, but would probably regret it. When the exit for Rte. 16 comes up, I take it and follow the directions to the Visitors Center. Hey, I thought the brochure said free parking, but this is gated and I have to get a ticket.

Different tour buses are lined up, each with a little kiosk to buy tickets. I wait in line at the orange and green Old Savannah Tours (same company as in St. Augustine, the one I didn't take and I wish I didn't take this one) and buy the trolley ticket plus ones for the museum, the Owens-Thomas House and the Isaiah Davenport House Museum. I'm also given a "Free Parking" coupon. (Ah, so it is free.) This trolley is already full, so I go in the museum, which is in an old train station. I wander around looking at all the artifacts and displays about the history of Savannah. There's an old locomotive and I take a couple of photos, but it has been painted over so many times, it looks terrible. There is an entire section on Girl Scouts as that organization started here. It's interesting to read what role women played during rough times and how they were the ones who often managed to raise money to support their men during war.

A Little History

Savannah was built on a high bluff along the Savannah River. It is Georgia's first "planned" city; designed in a series of grids focusing around 24 squares of which 22 remain. It was originally a place for England's working poor and to increase trade. Because General James Oglethorpe became friends with the Yamacraw Indians, there were never the war issues that other colonies suffered with the natives.

It is said that during the Civil War, General Sherman, when burning his way to the coast, found Savannah too beautiful to destroy. Instead, he offered the city to President Abraham Lincoln as a Christmas gift.

I finally have enough of this and head back outside. I consider walking to the end of the long building as there are old train cars, but decide to wait. I board the trolley and sit in the front seat just behind the driver. The trolley fills and we are off.

What a rattle trap! The vehicle jerks and groans and I wonder if the driver has ever driven this thing. We travel around the squares and after about Jack's fifth, "This is so and so square and on your right is the statue of so and so or the monument of blah blah," I am incredibly bored and discouraged. Yes, the squares are beautiful with fountains and big live oaks from which hang Spanish moss, but I didn't take a tour to look at statues. Some old homes are pointed out, but there is also quite a bit of newness to this old city (even a McDonalds.) It is interesting to see Paula Deen's restaurant, Lady and Sons. There are even Paula Deen tours.

The trolley winds around these squares and back. I'd been told that the stop for my house tours would be Stop 7. However, they'd made some changes to the route, which are not on the map, and Jack is confused. Next thing I know, he's announcing Stop 8, which is a shopping area. What happened to Stop 7? I hop off (well, as much hopping as hobbling with my walking stick will afford) and begin the trek back towards the two houses that I intend to visit.

There are some gorgeous structures in Savannah. Many are now restaurants, hotels, and private homes. The main entrances are up a flight of stairs and many of those are beautiful themselves. It's hard to get photos with all the trees. There are a few quiet streets, but for the most part, the roads are very busy with stop-and-go traffic. I find the Owens-Thomas House.

The tour starts in the Old Slave Quarters with a brief talk about slavery in Savannah then we walk over to the house. No photographs are allowed to be taken inside the house. The tour itself is basically about the family and the house; not really much history. I don't care about the furniture or who in the family owned what was in the cabinets. However, the architecture is wonderful. The kitchen and a huge cistern are in the basement, an area I find interesting. The walls were built of tabby and very thick. The house actually had three cisterns, one of the first places to have indoor plumbing; even before the White House. Most of the styles of building came from Europe where they had indoor plumbing.

The English Regency architecture (and I can't remember the term) is symmetrical. What is on one side is on another even if not real. For instance, there are matching . . . towers (I don't know the proper name) on both sides of the house and on the portico, there is the main entrance and two doors on the side into the towers; one to a butler's pantry and the other to the master bedroom. There is a window to one side and the indentation on the matching side; no real window, but keeping with the symmetry. Inside, the symmetry continues with fake doors and windows to offset the real ones.

The building is beautiful, though most of the furniture and set pieces inside are guesses as to what might have been there through the different periods. Upstairs is a Plexiglas section of floor to show the plumbing and part of the middle cistern. The other cistern is on the roof. The cisterns collected rain water and ran through lead pipes throughout the house. Yes, lead pipes. Good thing they didn't use the water for drinking.

Yellow fever was prevalent throughout many years in the south. Some years were much worse than others. Then came a year when the city was struck extremely hard and Savannah was put in quarantine for about three years. This was totally devastating for wealthy merchants relying on trade as nothing came in and nothing went out. Many, if they lived, lost most of their families and their fortunes. Possessions were sold off and eventually houses.

Back outside where I am allowed to take pictures, I do. Then it is off to find the Davenport House. A tour is already in progress, but Gayle volunteers to take me on a private tour. How lucky is that! This house isn't as pretty on the outside as the other house. Georgian brick is called gray brick (not gray to me, but not the rusty red we think of in brick). The inside is fascinating. In restoring this home, they had researched period wallpapers and those were brilliant and stunning. Again, most all the original furniture and even fireplaces had been sold off, so it was decorated with pieces that could have been in a house like this. What was fortunate was that they were able to get back a couple of the original Italian marble fireplaces with the original bill of sale. Even though Georgia has its own marble quarries, it was more fashionable to have Italian marble.

Gayle picks up a glass ball saying it's an early fly catcher. I know exactly what it is! I saw one on television the other night while watching "American Pickers." The glass has a hollow wick coming up from the bottom in which sugar can be put inside and when the flies get in, they can't get out. They have them for sale in the gift shop and I'll buy one on the way out.

The molding in this building is beautiful, intricate; handmade of horsehair plaster, but the thing that has me drooling is the spiral staircase going up three floors. Oh, what I wouldn't give to be able to photograph that! Again, there's a term for this, but I cannot remember . . . it's not totally free standing . . . and Gayle can't remember, but it's only attached on one side to the wall and the floors. She won't let me take photos and says I'll have to settle for a post card. I suppose if I even try to take a photo when her back is turned, the big, black guard following us probably would smack me to the ground.

The tour ends in a lovely walled garden. Across the way, I can see a Dick Blick Art Supply Store. I buy most of my art supplies from Blick. Gayle says it's a new store recently opened this past fall. Should I go? I really don't need any more art supplies.

In the gift shop, I purchase a couple of post cards of that staircase. They had taken the photo looking down and it's all the brown wooden treads. An okay picture, but I would have taken it looking up with the white walls and blue. Looking up is a stunning view of the spiral. My mind is so focused on that staircase that I forget to buy that fly catcher.

The next trolley that comes along is crowded with only one seat left with a young woman. Luckily it's a front seat. I feel bad crowding her. At least this trolley doesn't sound like it's going to fall apart. Lillie announces that this is Stop 9. Then again, she keeps getting confused as to the number because of those new changes.

As we go through the stops getting back to #1, we do a section of the River Street District which is a lot of shops. My seat mate tells me I have to go there and visit the Peanut Shop where they have all kinds of nuts with free samples. Ooh, I like nuts. I see other things to make me want to return. There are photos to take that cannot be achieved from a trolley.

Finally back where the tour began, I head to where I'd earlier seen some train cars. It's called the Whistle Stop Café, but wouldn't you know, it's closed for renovations. It looks like there's part of the café in a building to one side and dining in the passenger car or on the outside platform at café tables. I wander onto the platform and take a few photos of the old, but renovated buildings. Then I see a sign that says Train Museum. Oooh, what's there?

The ramp leads outside. What? There's nothing here. Then I look across the street. OH MY GOD! (Gosh, I've been saying that a lot lately.) There was a huge, HUGE area with trains and roundhouse and buildings and . . . but it's getting late. I need to get a hotel room. I'm babbling to myself, but, maybe I can walk over and take a peek.

Georgia State Railroad Museum

The Central of Georgia Railroad was chartered in 1833 and "is believed to be the largest and most complete Antebellum railroad repair facility still in existence in the world" with a partial roundhouse still remaining and a working turntable. Some buildings destroyed by fire have been rebuilt. In 1926, half the roundhouse was redesigned to accommodate bigger engines. The floor of the roundhouse is made up of wooden blocks to absorb shock, weight, grease, oil, and ash.

The entrance is through the gift shop. It costs $9 and is good for six days. Okay, I can look around a little and come back tomorrow. I head out into the yard. Every step is a wow. This is the first intact turntable (really the only) I've ever seen and there are engines and cars in every space in the roundhouse.

Turn Table

Huge arches lead to other areas. Wow, wow. I enter areas that used to contain garden, blacksmith shops, machine shops and more. Most of what remains are brick walls and rooms with story boards telling about each area. Section after section and out back was a HUGE 125-foot smokestack. I am slack jawed and close to drooling. What a fantastic place! I take lots of pictures.

So Much to Explore

I leave without seeing it all. The girl at the counter says that during the day they have tours. I am definitely coming back! I turn in my "Free Parking" coupon at the gate and I'm given directions to the Comfort Suites on West Bay Street. The hotel is next to the ramp to the I-17 Talmadge Memorial Bridge. I'm given room 314 and in returning the trolley to the lobby, I go outside to get photos of the bridge. I'm almost underneath it. I don't often get to see this view of a bridge.

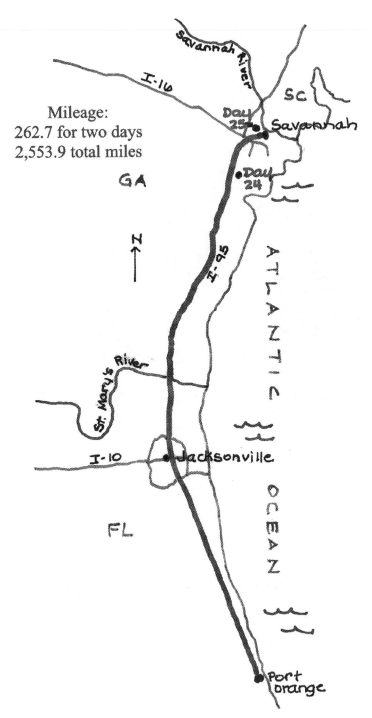

Port Orange, Fla. to Savannah, Ga.; two nights, two different hotels

DAY 26, FRIDAY, FEBRUARY 15

Savannah, Part 2

In looking over the invoice for the hotel, they not only charge $6.23 room tax, $5.34 city/county tax, and $1 occupancy tax, but they also charge $5 for parking. What's with that?

A message pops up on the computer from Gayle Hedrington, a friend from Croydon, N.H., asking what hotel I'd stayed the night before because she thinks she is near the Applebees that I'd written about in the blog. I am beside myself with excitement. How awesome to be on separate trips (she and her sister, Judy Guarno, had gone to New Orleans) and manage to hit the same city at the same time heading towards home. We are both train enthusiasts and as I'd visited that wonderful museum and planned to return, (my ticket is good for six days) it would be awesome if we could meet up. She'll love that museum! We arrange to meet at the Visitor Information Center (VIC) at 10 a.m.

I hurry the packing and check out of the hotel. The sky is sunny and clear with the temperature at 52 degrees. It feels warmer than the day before, but that's probably due to the sun and no overcast. I arrive at the VIC 15 minutes early. Not a big deal as I enjoy looking around. They have further to come than I. I park where they will be able to see my vehicle and license plate when they pull in. I put on my sweater. Poor thing is getting so raggedy-looking with all the pulled threads. I'd forgotten to ask Gayle which car they are using, but when I see one with New Jersey plates, I know it has to be them. They don't see my vehicle and are driving by when Gayle notices me on the sidewalk.

I am so happy to see someone I know! I hobble over to their car to give a warm greeting. "Wow, look at all those beads!" The car has strands and strands hanging on the rearview mirror and seats. Well, they'd just come from New Orleans and it is Mardi Gras season. We hug and chat about our trips as we head for the train museum.

Gayle and Judy are as impressed with the trains as I. We look around and I show them areas I'd visited the day before. We are in time for a little tour which includes a train being driven from its "home" in the roundhouse onto the turntable then out on a track where passengers can climb up a set of steps to get into an open car. The engine pushes the car back onto the turntable where it moves around to another set of tracks and we are pushed off and down the tracks. A young man talks about the train yard and a little history of the trains in Savannah. Unfortunately, it's hard to hear him with two little kids yapping nearby.

The engine pulls us back onto the turntable, the table turns, and we are pushed out onto another set of tracks for a short distance where information about the rail yard is explained. At one time, this train yard was enormous. It is huge now with what remnants are left, but there was a lot more back in the day. This was a major confluence for repairs and there was much coming and going of trains.

After getting off the train, Judy goes to check on her dog. I am taking my time with photos when one of the workers that Gayle had been speaking with earlier points out an engine from the Claremont-Concord Line.

Concord-Claremont Engine

We are excited. The Concord-Claremont line was in New Hampshire and came through Bradford where I now live. Of course, we have to see that! The engine is in the roundhouse behind a No Admittance sign. We are trying to get good shots of it and capture the logo without a lot of I-beams and debris in the way when another man comes up and offers to let us in the restricted area. How awesome is that! Gayle says it's because she dares to talk to people. She's always telling me I need to be brave and speak up.

Brian Spokes says they haven't had this engine long and repairs are needed. We are excited to find something here from back home. Gayle says we now have pictures we can use for our respective jobs (besides for our train collection photos) as she works for a radio station and I for a newspaper. Du'uh, I wouldn't even have thought of that if she hadn't mentioned it.

Judy hasn't come back and even though she told Gayle to take her time, we figure we should go. This is an awesome place to visit, but even I am ready to move on although there's more to see. We discuss lunch, but I don't want to drive anywhere yet as I want to visit the water district on the trolley. With hugs all around, we part ways. It was so wonderful to spend time with them. I am very happy. There aren't too many with whom I can share my enthusiasm for trains. I just can't get over the three of us ending up in Savannah at the same time. What are the odds?

On to the Riverfront

With reluctance, I do the same trolley tour as it's only half price on the second day. I end up sitting third from the back as the car is crowded. The lady across from me asks how I liked the tour yesterday and I give my honest opinion. She hopes we have a better driver today and we do.

The stop I want is an hour into the tour. Cindy is a phenomenal tour guide and although she talks about the squares and statues, she flavors it with entertaining stories. The back curtain of the trolley is up and many pictures are taken of structures and architecture to show more of what Savannah is like. Today's ride is enjoyable. At one stop a couple sits down in front of me. Her perfume is so overpowering, I feel sick. Even though we're supposed to stay seated while the trolley is moving, I get up and take the last seat, which is now empty.

Many buildings along the route catch my eye. Here are some of how I pictured Georgia homes would look with their two story balconies and elaborate staircases leading to the main entrance. Today I even enjoy the squares and take many pictures knowing that most will never be ones good enough to use. I am particularly taken by a storefront which we are told was once a Ford dealership. The windows and architecture are beautiful and ornate with the top frame of the window coming to a peak and the row of them reminding me of the swag icing on a cake.

The story told by the tour guides is that this was one of Henry Ford's first dealerships. It is said that he thought the Spanish moss would make excellent stuffing for the seat cushions. He didn't know that the moss is full of chiggers (little red bugs that bite) and needs to be treated before being used. Needless to say, it didn't take long for him to find something else with which to stuff the cushions.

The trolley goes down a steep cobblestone alley to River Street where I hop off onto uneven gray bricks and head down the sidewalk. A different trolley runs on tracks from one end of this street to the other where the driver then walks to the other end of the car and drives it back. Back and forth on the same line all day.

I check out the Peanut Shop. It's small and crowded with many bins and containers of different flavored nuts with free sample. It's interesting and fun, but nothing I'd care to purchase. At a large market across the street and I wander between the tables looking at the wares. I almost buy a pair of earrings to be able to say I bought something, but nothing really catches my eye. The other stuff is mostly tourist-type items. I re-cross the street and get a burger and fries at One Eyed Lizzie's. It's okay. They put mustard on the burger and that's all I can taste.

I meander down to the end of the storefronts then turn around and head back, going past the trolley stop. There are some interesting passageways between this level and East Bay Street which is 42 feet above River Street. I would not want to climb the many steps nor walk up the steep inclined sidewalk. (To the original settlers, where the main street is now was a bluff overlooking the river.)

I again cross the street to get photos along the river of the tour boats, tug boats, and a huge freighter under the Eugene E. Talmadge Memorial Bridge (the bridge which will later take me into South Carolina.) A couple sit at a bench I am approaching and they have pinkish red drinks. I have to ask. The daiquiris come from a place across the street, there are many flavors to add, and they'll let you sample anything. Ooh, I have to try one.

Wet Willie's is a happening place. I am waited on right away. The drinks are made with 190 proof grain alcohol and the barkeep shows me a menu. I try the strawberry. Good, but not quite what I want. Oooh, this stuff is cold and my throat hurts. How about a pina colada? He says I can mix it with the strawberry and gives me a sample. Oh, yes, this is good. I order a small and take it out on the street as a lot of people are wandering around with drinks. It's not easy taking photographs with my walking stick in one hand and the drink in the other. I have to find a place to lean the stick and set the cup down. I manage just fine.

I slowly head back to the trolley stop and the next one has Jack for the driver. Oh, great (sarcasm.) He remembers me and I head to the back seat. His speaker is loud and the voice goes right through me. I hear more about the squares, statues, and monuments, blah, blah, blah. At least I only have to put up with him for four stops.

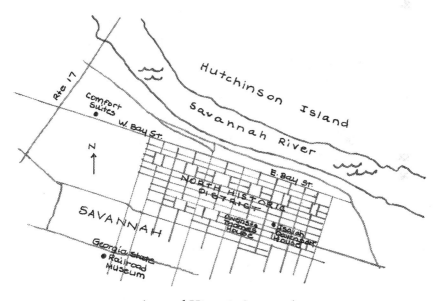

Around Historic Savannah

Back in the truck, I give the gate lady my get-out-of-jail-free card (free parking for trolley riders) and ask how to get to Rte. 17N. I'm ready to get out of Georgia. There are a couple places I would have liked to visit; that cemetery Janet Crocker recommended and a riverboat cruise, but I want to head north and it's getting late. It's time to go over that fabulous Talmadge Memorial

Bridge and try to take pictures by holding up the camera and hoping to get decent shots.

The Talmadge Memorial Bridge, spanning the Savannah River, is a cable-stayed bridge providing 185 feet of vertical navigational clearance. Savannah has the largest single ocean container terminal in the east and is the fourth busiest seaport in the nation. The bridge has a total length of 1.9 miles, carrying four lanes of traffic.

A Disappointing Hardeeville, S.C.

I cross into South Carolina and the scenery becomes . . . unremarkable. My goal is to find the first good hotel as it is 4 p.m. A little bit later, I come to Hardeeville, S.C., which has a row of hotels. This is the first area since crossing the state line that seems to have anything, but it's depressing and looks like it has seen better days. There's not much else here. I get the impression that at one time, this was a nice, busy town. Perhaps with I-95 nearby, this section of Rte. 17 now gets by-passed. I look for a Comfort Inn or Country Inn and pass through the business section without seeing anything of interest. I'd better turn around and take what I can get.

The first place back is a Travel Lodge. Their prices are cheap. How bad can the place be? The manager is very nice and has me sample his coffee, which is Starbucks. He admits to watering it down, which is the only way I'll drink that brand. He tells me what a hard time he is having keeping the place running. We chat about the economy and he offers to let me see the room first. I say no, I just want to get settled in. He insists. I fill out the card and take the key.

I'm so glad he insisted I check out the room. The place is downright gross! Things are in disrepair, it's dirty, and the cover to the toilet tank doesn't even go with that toilet. It's too small and sitting on the top at an angle. I go back to the office and apologize, saying the room isn't acceptable. I leave feeling like there are things crawling all over me. No wonder why he's having a hard time keeping the place running. No one in their right mind would stay here.

The next hotel is a Quality Inn. The ones I've seen in the coupon books are usually more expensive than I spend for a night, but after that last place, maybe something nicer will take away the feeling of creepy-crawlies. There are two floors and no elevators. I ask for a room on the first floor. You know what they say, "You get what you pay for." Turns out this place is an exception to other Quality Inns and it's just a step up from the Travel Lodge, but at this time of night, I don't want to search further. Had I read the name right on the sign? Didn't it say "Quality" Inn?

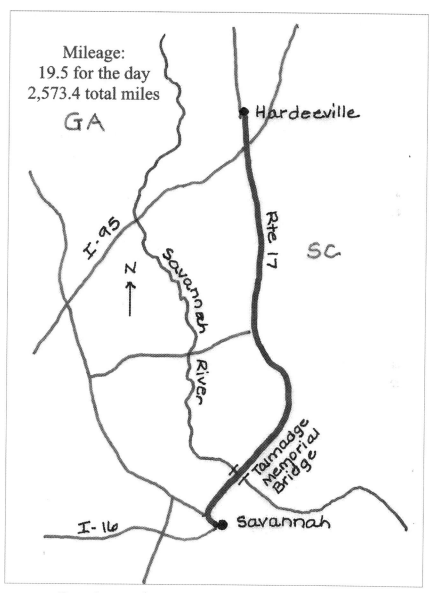

Mileage:
19.5 for the day
2,573.4 total miles
GA

Hardeeville

I-95

Savannah River

Rte 17

SC

N

Talmadge Memorial Bridge

I-16

Savannah

From Savannah to a Disappointing Hardeeville, S.C.

My room is on the back side of the pool and away from the office. Not bad, but that means the luggage trolley is far away at the front and I am not about to walk all that way to get it and then bring it back. Parking to the room is on the back side of the motel near the trees. To get to the room, I walk down a sleazy corridor, open on both ends between two sets of buildings under a connecting roof, past a filthy, noisy ice machine, beat up Coke machine and a bunch of dirty napkins on the cement walkway. In the front, my room is two doors down and faces a beautiful pool. Well, that's positive. Too bad it's too cold to swim.

Inside, the disappointment continues. This place isn't much better than the Travel Lodge; maybe a little cleaner. I make three trips back and forth to the truck. I turn on the a/c because the room is hot and stuffy. It quickly gets cold. I turn the temperature knob, but it still blows cold air. I finally shut it off figuring I'll have to turn it on during the night. I don't and I'm still cold.

I can't connect to the internet, call the front desk, and finally get connection. I have a good on-line chat with Karen who says she hasn't see kitty again, but Freyja is still eating. I try calling Adam and then Don to hear some friendly voices to distract me from this appalling room, but there's no answer at either place.

I can't wait to get out of this dump!

DAY 27, SATURDAY, FEBRUARY 16

Get Me Out of Here!

This crappy room won't let me sign onto the internet. I'm cold and not very happy. Yep, "You get what you pay for," and this is a cheap place. There's dust everywhere; TV, microwave, fridge, and the bathroom door has handprints all over it. At least the bed was clean and I slept fairly well.

As soon as this writing is finished, I'm heading for Charleston. It's about an hour and a half away. Today is a work day and I need to hole up. Hotel check-in usually isn't until 3 p.m., but I'm hoping to be able to do so earlier. I may stop somewhere if I see a place to visit just so I can kill some time. I'm on my last set of clean clothes, so laundry needs to be done, too. Perhaps I'll go back to the Comfort Suites Inn on the Ashley. I couldn't find my hotel coupon book for South Carolina last night.

Arrggh, let me get packed up and outta here!

Taking My Time Getting to Charleston

I check out of that crappy Quality Inn (hmph, some quality that was) and am on the road by 8:40 a.m. The skies are sunny with pale clouds, the temperature is 47 degrees and the odometer reads 15,739.9. I am glad to leave Hardeeville behind; a place where I never want to return.

Rte. 17 merges with I-95 for awhile and when the highway splits again, there is a visitors' center at Frampton Plantation; (not Peter.) This place has some gorgeous live oak trees of which I take photos. Inside, is a gift shop with the rooms crammed with stuff. It feels claustrophobic. The women behind the counter are in a deep conversation. One says the usual, "If we can answer any of your questions . . . ," but she has no heart in the greeting and I feel I'm intruding and not welcome. I do a quick look-see and it's the usual tourist items. It's so narrow, I'm afraid something will get knocked over. I grab hotel coupon book from the rack on my way back outside. I wander around and take more photos.

Very Little History

Research gives me very little. In 1862, General Robert E. Lee's troops built an earthen fortification here as a fall-back position for the defense of the Charleston to Savannah railroad. The original house and farm buildings were burnt by Sherman's troops in 1865. This current house was built in 1868.

It's warmer in the truck and I spend a few minutes looking at the brochures deciding where to stay for a couple days. Do I go back to the Comfort Suites West of the Ashley? It's familiar and I liked it or do I stay in North Charleston? I can't decide. I'm leaning towards the familiar and not being right in the city. I leave Frampton Plantation at 9:48 a.m. I might be able to finagle a room earlier, but feel I at least need to wait until 2 p.m. There will probably be places along the way to visit to kill some time.

Continuing north, I see a brown sign that indicates a point of interest. It pictures a pair of binoculars and says wildlife. Okay, let's see where that goes. I drive and drive and wonder if I am ever going to reach the end. I see turkeys and reach a marshy area where a few vultures are tearing up a Styrofoam to-go box. It seems funny to see that out in the middle of nowhere. I try to get photos of the birds flying off. The road continues on and there isn't any indication that it leads anywhere spectacular. I turn around.

Exploring along a Side Road

Edisto Nature Trail

The Edisto Nature Trail is in Jacksonboro and off the south-bound lane which means driving a little further north to get a place to change directions. There's a dirt parking area just off the highway. The narrow trail has boardwalks three planks wide over the wet areas. A sign says surveillance cameras are in use along the trails. That's odd. I put on my sweater, sling the camera over my shoulder, grab my walking stick, and head off. A little further in is a mailbox with trail maps which give good information about the area. It's hard to imagine that this was once farmland with all these trees and vegetation. The brochure states that from the age of the trees, the farm was abandoned in the 1940s. I look at the trees, bushes, and wetland and try to picture this as cleared land.

The trail moves into a swampy area and I read that part of this section was the Old King's Highway, the original road used by British troops between Savannah and Charles Towne (now Charleston) between 1670 and 1730. If the area looks spooky to me now with its current overgrowth after having been farmland for a number of years, I can't fathom how dense and dangerous it was in its original state. The hardships those men must have experienced blazing a trail through this had to be extremely difficult. The mosquitoes, alligators, snakes, and other nasties had to have been horrendous.

At a fork in the boardwalk, the path to the right, the Long Trail, has a sign announcing it is closed due to flooding. I'm disappointed as the map states there's an Old Phosphate Mine, canals, and an old railroad bed. I am out here all alone hearing only a few bird calls in the trees and don't want to take chances. It feels closed in with the narrow boardwalk and the vegetation creeping close. I take the left path trying to picture what it must have been like for those early peoples. It would have been horrible in a place like this in the summer when the humidity is atrocious and all kinds of terrors from the tiny no see-ums and ones not seen until too late can attack from any direction. I finish the trail just about noon.

Caw Caw Interpretive Center

The next wildlife place along Rte. 17 is Caw Caw Interpretative Center in Ravenel, again on the southbound side. It costs $1 to walk the trails; can't go wrong with that price. The temperature has risen to 53 degrees. I get a map in the gift shop and head out. From the Upland Forest Loop, I move out onto a long boardwalk overlooking old rice fields and bordering the only freshwater marsh in the park. It's still hard for me to get the concept of what rice fields looked like. The marsh grasses are tall and brown, however, this is not a good day for seeing birds and the only one is a kingfisher too far away for a good photo.

Off the boardwalk, the path meanders through the forest and then onto another boardwalk through a swamp. The first boardwalk was straight with sharp corners, whereas the Swamp Boardwalk curves around trees. The water below has that black-mirrored surface like at Cypress Gardens. I stop often to look over the railings and study the debris under the surface; yes, it's "too cold for alligators." Maybe that's a good thing as I'm out in the swamp alone. Oh, wait, there is someone else out on these trails and I stop to talk to a couple from Columbia, S.C. When I mention I'm from New Hampshire, she exclaims that she grew up in Plainfield and lived in Laconia awhile.

Swamp Boardwalk

I finish the walk through the swamp and come out to a hard packed trail big enough for a vehicle. It's nice and peaceful along here. The skies darken and it starts to sprinkle. I need to find my way back before it really rains. I am a lover of maps, but this one is confusing. I can't tell where I am and that song about Charley on the MTA keeps running through my head; "He'll never get off, oh, he'll never get off" only my tune runs, "She'll never get out, oh . . ." For once, I'm scared being out on a trail alone. It's not a comfortable feeling.

A couple of young women catch up with me and direct me to go back and take the first left (I would have thought I needed to go right; shows how my sense of direction is off.) They also turn around, but quickly outdistance me and disappear, leaving me alone once more. I catch up to two older guys and follow them across old rice fields where some of the grasses look like bamboo.

Quarter Drains

Rice was planted on raised earthen beds and the channels between were called quarter drains which circulated water through the fields. The fields were flooded after planting for the growing season and drained for harvesting.

The men stop and I keep going eventually making my way back to the truck at 1:30 p.m. What a relief! I can't get over being scared. (Later, in re-looking at the map, I realize that it doesn't show all the twists, turns and zigzags and that is how my sense of direction got skewed.) Twenty minutes later, I reach the Comfort Inn Suites. The temperature has dropped to 50 degrees and the odometer reads 15,838.4. The wind picks up and the air is very chilly. The woman behind the desk remembers me and apologizes, saying they have no rooms available. Oh, no! Now what? I get back in my truck and head towards downtown.

Back to the Familiar

Let me see if I can get into the Holiday Inn Riverside. That's the round hotel I stayed in before. On Rte. 17N just before the hotel, there is traffic merging from the right and then left lanes. I need to cross the two lanes merging from Rte. 61 on the left to get into the hotel entrance. Not an easy task with vehicles speeding along. I cut in front of someone off; I swear I can hear the curses.

By the time I pull up at the entrance, the sky is full of dark gray clouds, the wind is whipping across the parking lot and rain is pelting down, just short of being icy. The odometer reads 15,843.0 which is 103.5 miles for the day for a total of 2,676.9.

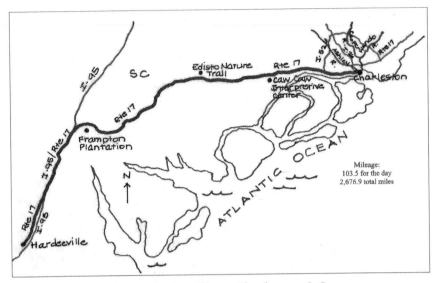

From Hardeeville to Charleston, S.C.

The guy at the counter spends quite a few minutes finding a space for me. There's some kind of wildlife event going on in town and all the hotels are booked. He says the only available room is a handicap. At this point, I'll take whatever. I need to get to work.

Unfortunately, there's an hour before the room will be ready and the price is $199; he cannot give me the coupon rate because of the special event in town. He writes on a piece of paper that he'll let me have the room for $139 and after tonight, the coupon rate. He can't sign me in, yet, but the room is mine. Whew, thank you.

I park the truck in the nearest slot I can find. It's a miserable walk back to the lobby. The wind threatens to blow me over and the rain feels like sleet. I am freezing. Maybe I should have put on my coat. I take the elevator up the fifteenth floor to wait my hour. The bar and restaurant are officially closed for the couple hours until dinner, but because of the number of people waiting, they are serving drinks. They make me a Mai Tai. After the day I've had, I really need it.

Megan brings my drink and remembers me from before recalling the very foggy morning I was trying to get photos. I say something about the day of the week and she says it's Saturday. I don't believe her. It can't be. It's only Friday, but in checking with someone else, I find it is Saturday. I panic. Oh, my God, Annette is going to kill me! I haven't done any work for the week and deadline is 5:30 p.m. She must be frantic wondering where I am. It can't be Saturday. How did I mess up the days of the week?

I head to the lobby after my allotted hour. People are trying to get checked in and everyone is being told that check-in isn't until 4 p.m. and it is only 3. There are a lot of unhappy folks. The woman behind the desk says my room won't be ready for a few more minutes. She also confirms that it is Saturday. Oh, no, again. Annette will be upset with me. I have got to get online and get work done.

Fifteen minutes later I am checked in and have the key for room 716. By then, all the spaces near the door and under the awning are full of cars. I squeeze a trolley past people unloading at the curb. At the truck, I cram everything I can into the two suitcases hoping nothing will blow away in the fierce wind. The truck is a mess. I load the trolley and begin the limp back through the wet parking lot. Thankfully the space isn't that far away, but still, my hair is dripping by the time I get inside. That freezing rain has me shivering. Someone says they are getting snow over towards Columbia.

The bed is only a full size. The bathroom is big to accommodate a wheelchair, but there is no vanity; no place to put my bag of essentials. The coffeemaker and other supplies are on little shelves. The work table is round, small, and maybe 24 inches in diameter. I can barely fit the laptop, a small notebook, pens and the mouse. (Good thing it's a trackball; I wouldn't have the room to move a regular mouse.) I put my box of other writing material on the other side of the table. I consider bringing in the table from the truck, which I'd brought in case I did any artwork, but this room isn't big enough.

First thing is to plug in the laptop and fire it up. I get out the cell phone, hoping it will work, so I can check in with Annette and apologize all over myself. She is gracious as ever. I can do my work this week on Sunday. I am so thankful. That taken care of, I finish unloading the trolley, take it back to the lobby, and returning to my room, the key won't work when I put it into the 714 slot. I try a number of times then check the room number. Whoops, I'm 716.

I rearrange the suitcases, put a small table that was near the TV in the bathroom to hold my essentials, and sign on to the computer to let everyone know where I am. There, that's taken care of. Now, I need sustenance; time to head back up to the restaurant. It's still too early for dinner, so I order another Mai Tai and take photos of the scenery. I can't get enough of these views. The rain has stopped and the sun is coming out.

Storm Clouds over Charleston

What an amazing view. In the far distance, a red and white freighter passes under the Ravenel Bridge. It looks like it's between the bridge and the top of the buildings of the city. I track its progress between the taller structures. The height of the hotel and angles and rise of the city make the freighter look out of place. I enjoy a delicious meal; sirloin steak, Caesar salad, and garlic mashed potatoes. I like it here a lot.

When I get back to my room, I check messages, post to Facebook and work an hour on the calendar until my headache worsens. I probably should have taken something earlier. I crawl into bed about 9:30. This is the smallest bed I've used in years. I worry I'll roll over and fall out during the night. Still, I fall asleep quickly and sleep well until about 3 a.m. when neighbors come slamming into their room. Not a big deal. I go back to sleep.

DAY 28, SUNDAY, FEBRUARY 17

A Day of Work

I'm re-grouping myself after being so messed up on the days of the week. From what I can tell, it started last Wednesday when I thought that was Valentine's Day. For someone who writes every day and has connections on the internet, I can't believe I got confused on the days of the week, especially for so many days. Then again, maybe I just messed up with yesterday.

It's nice to not have to climb over a tub wall to get in the shower. The curtain ends about eight inches from the bottom and water splashes out onto the floor. Good thing there are extra towels. Clean, refreshed, and full of a good breakfast, I settle in for serious work.

The day is spent in my room only breaking for a quick lunch at the restaurant. Two loads of laundry add to the busyness of the afternoon. That means going from the seventh floor to the laundry room on the first. There is only one washer and dryer. I get the work for the newspaper done, import 474 photos to the laptop, and edit 20. I've a long way to go.

By the time I retrieve the second load of clothes from the dryer, I am ready for another break. It is 5 p.m. and being a Sunday I am hoping that it's a shag night. I enjoyed that the last time I was here and would love a closer view. I quickly fold the shirts and leave the small clothes for when I return. Awww, no DJ in the lounge, no old folks dancing . . . that's disappointing. I sit at a table on the restaurant side and order a Mai Tai and Caesar salad, take photos of the view, and watch a couple freighters leaving the harbor beyond Fort Sumter.

Sasha Wolfe

A Story

Meckie, one of the waitresses, comes over and points out the window. "See that rubble out there; that mess just in front of that houseboat and sailboat? That's the remnants of another boat, all that's left," she says and goes on with a story.

Some years back, during hurricane season, a storm caused an exceptionally high-running tide which filled the marsh and flooded low-lying areas. The restaurant across the way looked like it was floating and people were stranded at the hotel because they could not get out to their cars in the parking lot. Many hung out at the restaurant and lounge watching the storm and some were having "a few too many." It was a good way to wait out a storm.

One of those guys was the owner of a shrimp boat and because of the high water, hadn't been able to tell how close to the marsh he anchored. As he continued imbibing his favorite beverage at the hotel, the tide went out leaving his boat mired in thick mud. The next morning, he and others went out and tried to pull his boat out of the muck. Nothing worked. After days and a lot of effort, all they could do was pull out the engine and other parts that would pollute the waters, salvage what they could, and abandon the vessel. The owner retrieved his cargo of shrimp and sold it, but that could not even come close to the loss of his boat.

Six years later, all that's left of the boat is that bit of rubble just showing above the water at low tide.

DAY 29, MONDAY, FEBRUARY 18

A Morning in Charleston

I get up just before 4 a.m. to use the bathroom and debate about staying up knowing that going back to bed at this time means I will end up sleeping past 5. I return to bed and it's almost 5:30 when I get up for the day. I settle at the laptop and write up the story Meckie told me last night. Then thinking about the sunrise from the restaurant, I quickly clean up, dress and hurry to the 15th floor. I am just in time although Brandi says I should've been there a few minutes earlier.

No problem, there are still some beautiful shots. I choose not to stay for breakfast. I'm not that hungry and I don't want to spend money on three meals a day. Plans for the day include more editing and posting of photos and a return to Middleton Place. Maybe the restaurant will be open. I'm fortunate to have the opportunity to get photos to replace the ones lost. The camellias are probably no longer in bloom, but maybe something else will be.

I edit 34 photos of Savannah. I usually take more landscape-oriented photos, but on this trip, I've taken more portrait ones. The emotions that run through me with that task, the things I want to tell you and show you are too many and I have to choose which will give the best glimpses into this city that mixes old with new. I edit, choose titles for each photo and make comments. I also know that when I do get to post the photos, there will be other thoughts and words that will come forth. Too many times there are no words to describe what I see. Sometimes I go back to the text pages to make additions.

It's getting on to 9 a.m. Time for an adventure.

Return to Middleton Place

The day is a sunny, chilly 50 degrees when I leave the hotel at 9:25 a.m. There's between half and a quarter of gas in the tank. I wait for a break in the traffic, zip across three lanes, and take an immediate right onto Rte. 61 for a series of street lights after street lights. When Rte. 61 veers to the left, I stop at that Rite Aid I'd visited the very first time I came this way.

I arrive at Middleton Place at 10:10 a.m. It's 45 degrees, I put on sweater and coat, pay $25 to walk the grounds, and head out. I take a different direction than when I was here before. I walk out to the Reflecting Pool and take photos of two swans.

Swans Reflected

It's wonderful to walk down paths while soaking in the natural beauty and hearing nothing but bird song. I am surprised and pleased that the camellias are still blooming. I can't resist taking photos. They've become my favorite flower.

After meandering through that garden, I wander out towards the Cypress Swamp and through the Bamboo Grove. I always used to think, like with rice, bamboo all came from China. This grows at least three times my height and can be as thick in diameter as my wrist. It grows so close together that no one can get through without the sharpest of machetes or big power tools.

The sun creates many shadows on the paths and even though it's warm on this cold morning, I prefer less sun for taking pictures. Still, I snap away. I come out to flooded rice fields and the Ashley River following along the path with the water on the left and the New Camellia Garden with its graveled almost 90 degree straight paths between the rows of bushes on my right. It's like looking down a tunnel with dropped petals creating spots of bright color. Occasionally, I meet up with other people or they would catch up and bypass me. I am a slow walker with these short legs and limp.

It's probably too cold for alligators. Wait! Aha! The light bulb goes off in my brain. What a wonderful title for my book. "Too Cold for Alligators" should be an attention getter. I like it. After all, I've heard it said enough on this trip.

Middleton Place is beautiful. I skirt the edge of symmetrical, more manicured gardens. This time of year there are few flowering plants besides the camellia. I could stay on the path along the water's edge and come out on the other side of the lawn by the Rice Mill, but I want to see the view from the top of the lawn. I hesitate. I've walked up stairs and down, up hills and down and I'm not sure if I want to make this next climb. With the help of the walking stick, I make the ascent up the grassy slope stopping on one of the tiers to admire the views. The expanse of green lawn, green of the palmettos, the gray-brown of the massive live oaks and the grayish Spanish moss, the murky blue of the river, the bright blue of the sky, the brick red buildings, and the camellias in reds, pinks, and white overtake the senses. The beauty and colors are astounding. I want to move in and be here every day.

Drawing closer to the house, the paths and gardens give way to a huge expanse of lawn extending from the river to the house. The top is sectioned in large tiers. I look towards the house. The long path from the river leads straight to a set of stone steps climbing to emptiness with a large pile of brick rubble off to the right with more signs of destruction on the left. The building that once sat here must have been amazing. There's a huge house on the far left partly shaded by live oaks on both sides. To the far right also shaded by trees are the ruins of another building.

The house that's standing was originally the south flanker which was built for gentlemen guests. Flankers were buildings adjacent to the main house. The three-story Big House (as the main houses were called) and the north flanker (which housed the library, conservatory, and ballroom) were burned by Union troops in 1856 and the gutted walls were later leveled during the Great Earthquake of 1886. The beautiful walls currently around much of the property were built using these bricks.

One of the lower tiers contains the Butterfly Lakes because of the two ponds each in the shape of a butterfly wing with a grassy walkway between. Smaller tiers lead from there down to the river.

After taking in the sights from the upper level, I make my way down to the Rice Mill taking the trail beyond the building. I hadn't traversed this trail a couple weeks ago. This is called the Azalea Hillside and in a few weeks, thousands of azaleas will be in bloom. There are a lot of stairs; their rise is often tall and steep which makes it difficult for me. The trail continues along a ridge above the Rice Mill Pond. I photograph the chapel and spring house across the pond, which is very picturesque, and at the bridge, I let a couple pass me because they would be faster than I. They stop on the bridge and look and take pictures. Not a big deal, as I will stop and take pictures, too. I am patient. But they stand there and look some more. The guy glances back at me waiting my turn. I swear he lingers just to be a jerk. He has a kind of arrogant smirk on his face. Jeez, what's with that.

They finally move on and I get my turn seeing the views from the bridge. I take a couple pictures before moving on myself. A cat comes to say hello and we have a conversation. I speak and he meows. A final flight of stairs and up an incline (inclines are easier for me than stairs) and I come out next to the restaurant. Hmmm, it's just about noon, but first I want to check on a house tour and find that the 12:30 tour is full. That's okay. I don't really need to see the inside.

After more photos, I go inside the restaurant and have a Caesar salad and a glass of water after which I stop to photograph that old gas pump that I was so excited about the first time I was here. I saw one on an episode of "American Pickers" on TV and now know how it worked. I next meander through the stable yard. There are horses, sheep, goats, cows, chickens, peacocks and a couple water buffalo. (*Water buffalo were first brought to Middleton Place in the late 18th century as an experimental draft animal.*)

Sheep and goats are used to "mow" the lawns. Also there are areas set up like little shops to show the various trades needed in the days of plantation life. There were displays and/or demonstrations in blacksmithing, pottery, carpentry and coopering, tanning, corn grinding, candle making, and spinning and weaving. Plantations had to be self-sufficient.

I visit the former slave quarters of which there is only the one left.

The originals were burned by the Union soldiers. This particular building was built around 1870 for freed slaves. After the war, some former slaves stayed on the plantations continuing to work for the planters. They often took on the last name of their employers. It wasn't easy for the freed slaves. They were free in name only. They were still discriminated against, still had trouble finding jobs, and often could not buy property even if they had money.

Passing back by the house, I pause at a set of brick steps with an iron gate at the top. This once led to the Big House destroyed during the Civil War. The brick walkway on the other side of the gate shows how the hallway ran through the original house from one portico entrance to the other with a view to the Ashley. This allowed cross ventilation in humid weather. Inside to the left is a pile of bricks, remnants of the original house.

Steps to the Fallen

I follow the carriage road past the ruins of the north flanker and veer off on another garden path past more open views on the right and rows of camellias and azaleas on the left. Some gardens are laid out in a grid pattern with straight paths often crisscrossing. I even like some of the flowers that had dropped to the ground and the many petals create bright spots of color in the old brown leaves and along the graveled paths.

There is part of me that totally enjoys the aloneness and quiet of a solitary walk. Sometimes, like when I see older couples strolling along holding hands, I feel a bit lonely. At these times, I wish I had a gentleman friend to share my adventures. Unless I stop to talk to a stranger, and I do occasionally, I have no one with whom to discuss the exact moments of wonder and discovery.

I find myself back at the Reflecting Pool and make my way to the parking lot. It's 1:45 p.m. and the temperature is 53 degrees. Driving back into Charleston, I realize I am sick of the traffic, the multiple-lane highways, and the speed. Drivers need to be more courteous and tolerant of one another with merging lanes and turning traffic (and out-of-staters who don't know where they're going or what lane to be in.)

Back at the Holiday Inn, the odometer reads 15,875.6 adding 32.6 miles to the journey for a total of 2,676.9.

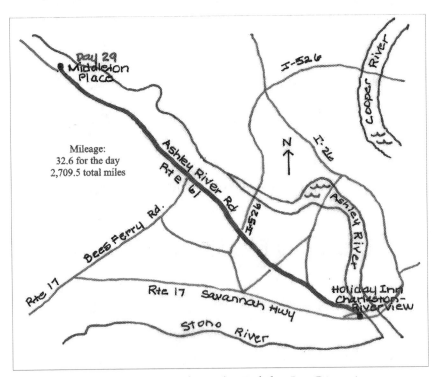

To Middleton Place from the Holiday Inn Riverview

I settle in my room and import the 310 photos I took at Middleton Place. I still have the ones I edited earlier to upload to Facebook. I'm a few days behind. I know, what's new. I am glad I returned to Middleton Place. It is amazingly beautiful. Even with two visits, I didn't see and experience everything. There are many trails not taken. I would go back again and again.

I am sitting in the restaurant enjoying a couple of Mai Tai's and a Caesar salad with grilled chicken when it hits me. I'm ready to go home. The thought brings tears to my eyes. Yes, I've been homesick off and on, but I wasn't ready to return to the cold and snow. I'm ready now. I'm done. I have a couple more stops in mind while making my way north, but the switch has been flipped. The leisureliness of the trip is over. I'm going home.

DAY 30, TUESDAY, FEBRUARY 19

Leaving Charleston Again

I get up this morning still with the feeling that I'm done and it's time to head home. I had said I'd be gone 30 days and at this point, it's been 30 days. It feels like I've been gone a long time. I've never been away from home this long.

The plans are to visit Boone Plantation this morning and maybe Fort Moultrie, which is across the river from Fort Sumter. Those two places are in Mount Pleasant just north of Charleston. I'm not sure where that will put me for the night. The next big decision is whether to stay on Rte. 17N until I reach Rte. 66W, which will take me through Virginia to Rte. 81N, or get on I-95N until Rte. 66. The first will be a little more leisurely with speed limits of 55 to 60 mph. It will also allow for some photo ops as there are places where I can pull over if the traffic isn't bad. The other way would be quicker at 70 mph, but I-95 is so boring. The decision won't need to be made until tomorrow.

I go up to the restaurant to get sunrise photos from this view for the last time. There is an amazing row of dark clouds on the horizon. Brandi says it's supposed to rain later today. I hope I'll still be able to visit Boone. I have the buffet breakfast; a few home fries, a couple pieces of bacon, cantaloupe and honeydew chunks, and one biscuit with a little gravy. The view, as always, is spectacular and the photos should be great with the sun coming out from behind the clouds over the historic district.

Now it's time to finish packing up and head out. I like this room. It's not perfect and there's not much space, but it's me – imperfect. The traffic is heavy, but maybe by the time I leave, all the work people will have arrived at their destinations. The route will take me through the city proper and I don't look forward to three lanes of heavy traffic in one direction with crossroads and then figuring out which exit off the bridge . . . that big, scary bridge . . . to get onto the island of Mount Pleasant.

I am out of the Holiday Inn by 8:50 a.m. The skies are cloudy with patches of blue, the temperature is 58 degrees, and there's a quarter of a tank of gas. It feels warmer than yesterday. As heavy as the traffic has been all morning, when I pull out of the parking lot, there isn't a vehicle in sight. That's good timing, as right by the hotel there are two other highways converging onto Rte. 17N along with vehicles trying to exit from the Holiday Inn. I cross the Ashley River and head into the modern part of Charleston.

It isn't a big deal, just lots of lights and traffic. Then there are the ramps; up, under, over, up and staying to the left, then right with other highways veering off both left and right and still Rte. 17N climbs. There it is. The Arthur Ravenel Jr. Bridge and it's up and up further. I pick up the camera and randomly shoot hoping to catch something. (Wish I realized I could do this on the way south.) Halfway across at the apex of the bridge, I cross into Mount Pleasant. Then it's down the other side and I am over the Cooper River.

Goodbye Charleston

The exit for Fort Moultrie and Patriot Park is the next right, but I want to go to Boone Hall Plantation first. That would be a left turn and figure it should be "just up the street." I drive and drive. The traffic is heavy. My original goal of visiting the plantation then Fort Moultrie isn't working out as time and the miles pass. I was under the impression that they were near one another. They are not and I am not going to backtrack.

Boone Hall Plantation

Boone Hall

I reach the plantation at 9:20 a.m. The temperature has risen to 61 degrees. The guy at the ticket booth at the entrance is very nice and we chat as I pay my entrance fee. Unlike the other places, the one fee covers everything; no extra charges for house tour, coach tour, or any of the talks. I drive towards the plantation house, but have to pull over and stop for photos. Here is the famous, three-quarter-mile Avenue of Oaks and it is gorgeous! A scene in "Gone with the Wind" was filmed here, although most the movie was made elsewhere. Other TV shows and movies also had scenes shot here such as "Days of Our Lives," "America's Most Wanted," "The Notebook," "North and South" and many more.

The parking signs are weird, all saying Additional Parking. I never see a spot that just says Parking. I stop near a small cotton field. I am later told it's used for demo purposes; planted every year and harvested in the spring. This is the closest I've ever come to one. What an amazing plant. It reminds me how a popcorn kernel pops. Signs say Do Not Pick Cotton Due to Boll Weevil Beetles. The song runs through my head, "Oh, when them cotton balls get rotten, you can't pick very much cotton in them old cotton fields back home . . ." I would like to see how they turn cotton into fabric.

Cotton Close Up

The temperature feels warm. Perfect weather for walking about except the sky is totally gray. A cool breeze comes up. (At least today's photos won't have shadows.) The woman at the Information and Tour Schedules little house says the coach will be leaving in about 15 minutes and I will need a coat as it gets cold out along the perimeter of the property. I go back to the truck for the sweater. The coach pulls up to its stop as I'm heading in that direction. I can see it behind a rundown building that's shored up with timbers and staging. I take the shortest route cutting around the back of that building and across a lawn instead of walking along the roadway and have time to take photos to add to my Abandoned and Windows collections.

That first step onto this open air coach is a doozy as I have all I can do to get my leg up that high. I have to physically pull myself up using the handrails. I sit in the front L-shaped seat facing forward. As more people get on, a woman from San Diego sits on the side of the seat that faces to my left. I was hoping no one would sit there. She blocks my view. The driver, across the aisle, is actually two seats back from me (with no seats in front of him.) That is weird.

As we ride along, Bob not only talks about the history, but explains how the farm operates today. They use a system called plastic gardening (not sure I hear the term right.) The plastic is 1 ml thick, comes in five-foot-wide rolls and fits into a tractor attachment. As the tractor drives along, it makes a raised bed in the soil and lays down the strip of plastic. Workers come along and do the planting by hand. (I don't know if they poke the holes in the plastic for the plants or if the hole is already there.) The plastic protects the plants and all the nutrients and irrigation is held in better. Bob says that production increased significantly with this type of gardening.

He also talks about the various vegetables grown here . . . just about anything and what's great is that they have produce growing all year; different vegetables or fruits for each season. Strawberries have to be replanted every year because the heat of the summer kills off the plants.

Boone Hall Plantation is one of the oldest working farms in America and known for its farm to table produce. Produce harvested here is sold at Boone Hall Farms Market further up Rte. 17. Out of about 5,000 acres, the current family still owns 738.

The plantation changed hands many times. The original planter was the second son of a wealthy British family. The rules back then said that only first sons inherit, so the second son moved to Barbados hoping to make his fortune there. When King Charles II was giving land grants in what is now South Carolina, Major John Boone left Barbados and came here where he was given something like 200 acres. He eventually married a wealthy local landowner's daughter and was awarded more acreage as part of the dowry.

His son, Captain Thomas Boone planted the ¾ mile, two rows of 88 evenly spaced live oak trees which line the sides of the carriage drive to the home. It took over 200 years for the tree canopy to meet overhead creating the scenic oft-photographed corridor.

The old rundown building that I'd photographed earlier was originally the Cotton Gin House. Bob says that the "gin" in cotton gin was actually a shortened term for engine. The building is being repaired to become a restaurant and gift shop.

The cotton gin was developed by Eli Whitney in 1793. Its purpose was to separate seeds from the cotton fibers using a combination of wire screen, small hooks, and brushes. The cotton was processed into material and seeds were used for growing more cotton, producing cottonseed oil or meal. This invention made possible the production of more cotton and the demand for slaves increased.

Early law stated that the land the king granted had to be used to send produce back to England. Cotton was the best choice, though indigo and rice were also popular. Slaves were needed to help clear the land and it took many years and eventually the property had over 5,000 acres. Rice was a poor crop for this plantation because the Wampacheone Creek is tidal and the waters too brackish. Brick making became the main focus besides the cotton and Boone Hall Plantation became known for its bricks; bricks that were used in the building of Fort Sumter and many other area structures.

After the Civil War, when there were not enough slaves to operate big plantations, acreage was sold off and other means had to be established for making money. Planters lost fortunes. A subsequent owner planted a pecan grove.

Pecans were the major crop by 1870 followed by cattle and cotton. The pecan is the largest of its genus and one of the longest living deciduous trees. Many trees were destroyed by hurricanes with Hurricane Hugo doing the worst damage in 1989.

As we travel around on this bumpy ride, Bob points out areas of interest like the fields now used for Civil War reenactments, the one used for a huge corn maze every year, and the places used for Halloween and other events. He mentions that the forests we now see had once been cleared for fields. I ask about the thick vines that grow everywhere. He says it is wisteria and explains that plantation owners would send all over the world for various plants, never realizing the harm some could cause. Wisteria vines are very destructive to other plants.

After the coach tour, I wander down Slave Road where there are nine original former slave quarters. Each has video, recordings, artifacts and storyboards of the lives of slaves. It was illegal in South Carolina to teach slaves to read and write. It is believed that these nine, because they are brick, housed the skilled slaves such as cooks, house slaves, carpenters, blacksmiths, etc., and the other slaves had wooden buildings closer to the fields.

Slave Row

I follow a road down to the Cotton Dock where cotton bales and produce were loaded onto barges to be taken to Charleston. Depending on tides, that could take up to twelve hours. The current building and dock on the Wampacheone Creek is a reproduction of an older building that was destroyed by a hurricane.

By this time, the wind has picked up something fierce. It feels like my hair is blowing straight up in the air. I get back to the Big House just in time for a tour. The current building was built 1933-35 on the site of the original plantation house. We only get to see five rooms on the main floor because the current owners still use the rest of the house. Wow, what a house! Pam explains that it was important that the planters prove their wealth by displaying impressive pieces. Although a lot of the original furnishings are gone, the place has been filled with items that would depict the typical eras. Two things that stand out in my mind are the cantilevered staircase and the 11-foot free standing mirror.

One of the stories is that a rich man from Canada bought the place and put in a cellar. No one told him that basements are not feasible in Low Country. Needless to say, the cellar flooded. There is a small area where there is still a wine cellar and we get a glimpse (couldn't see much) down those stairs.

Back outside, I wander for a short distance along the river, but the tide is out and it's not very picturesque. I next stroll through the gardens enjoying the vibrant flowers in bloom. I take photos all around the house. No photos could be taken inside, of course. I finally make my way back to the truck just as it starts raining. It's 12:15 and the temperature has risen to 65 degrees.

Shallotte, North Carolina

As I drive north on Rte. 17, the temperature fluctuates between 57 and 60 degrees. The North Carolina border is crossed at 2:45 p.m. Periodically I try taking pictures on the move. The landscape becomes more brown with less green; like winter without snow.

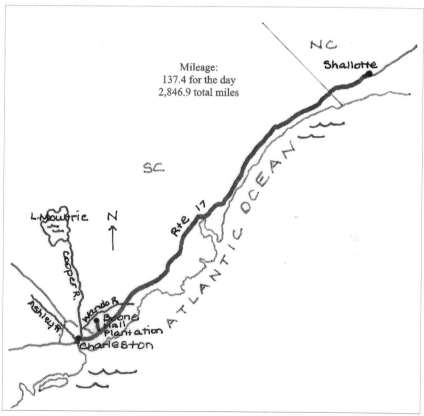

From Charleston to Shallotte, N.C.

In Shallotte, (pronounced with a long o) I stop at a Golden Corral for a buffet dinner. It's too salty. Further up the road, I pull off the highway for the night. The odometer reads 16,013; 137.4 miles for the day for a total of

2,846.9. This stay at a Comfort Inn is a disappointment. For the most part, the room is okay, but right off the bat, I notice filthy child-like hand prints all over the TV screen. I go out to the desk and she gives me a special cloth telling me not to put any water on it. It doesn't work. The screen is sticky. I call and she comes to the room. She has to put a little water on the cloth to get the screen clean.

She leaves and I sit in the chair. Ew, the arms are full of that sticky stuff, too. Ugh, gross! In looking at other things, I wonder if the coffee pots and coffee makers are ever cleaned with detergent and water or just rinsed out. Then I can't sign on the internet and have to call a special number. He calls back and connection is soon established. Good, I can get a little work in before bed.

DAY 31, FEB. 20

Out of North Carolina

This morning I find another issue with the room while brushing my teeth. The sink won't drain. Oh, I am so ready to be out of here, but I need to make a decision. Do I make my way to Fredericksburg, Va. up Rte. 17N, which is the way I came down, or do I take Rte. 40 out of Wilmington and make my way to I-95N? Would that be a quicker way to Virginia?

Google maps says the quickest way is to take Rte. 40W to Rte. 117 and onto Rte. 795 to I-95N. It'll take five hours. Well, more adventures ahead, I see. In checking out, I tell the desk clerk about my issues with the room and she gives me an extra 15 percent off. I appreciate that. Now I feel better about the experience.

With the gas tank at three-quarters full, I am on Rte. 17N by 8:55 a.m. It is sunny and 48 degrees. The highway is elevated over wetland areas. I cross the Cape Fear River into Wilmington and exit onto Rte. 40 reaching Rte. 795 at 11:10 and Rte. 95 twenty minutes later. At noon, I stop at the Nash County Rest Stop to use the facilities. I cross into Virginia at 1:40 with the temperature at 50 degrees. I hold the camera up a few times and snap pictures. I don't know if they will come out. For the most part, the drive isn't bad, mostly tedious. There are periods when there aren't any other vehicles around me and that feels good. Other times vehicles are passing on both sides and sometimes they're just barely going the speed limit. I find myself tense and gripping the steering wheel so hard that my arms ache and have to shake and wiggle in my seat a little bit to get muscles to relax

Heavy black smoke can be seen about a mile away and as I get closer, it's a big fire on the side of the road in the southbound lane. There are people all around and emergency vehicles. As I drive past, it looks like a tractor trailer exploded. All that's left is the cab and a trail of flaming debris. I hope no one was injured. I pass through Richmond and wonder what it would be like to explore. There must be tons of history here. I hold up the camera again to snap a couple photos and think, perhaps another time.

A stop is made in Petersburg, Va. for gas. It's the cheapest I've seen all day at $3.67/gal. Most stations are over $3.70 and many closer to $3.80. It is almost 1:20 p.m., 47 degrees. Forty minutes later, I pass through most of Fredericksburg and get off of I-95 onto Rte. 17N. There I find a Comfort Suites and decide to call it a day. It was a long six hour drive covering 347.3 miles for a total of 2,846.9.

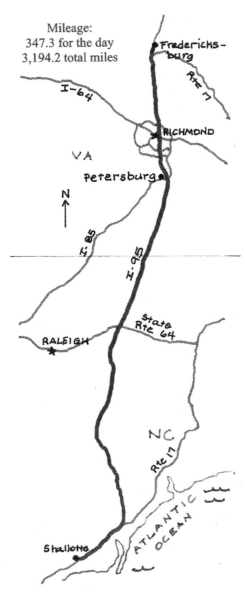

Fredericksburg, Va.

Elevator two in this place creaks and groans. I keep waiting for the floor to drop out. It scares me. Someone from the third floor says that elevator one is haunted. I think she's wrong and it's elevator two. I receive word from home that another big storm is due in this weekend. I'll have to pay close attention because the last thing I want to do is to be driving in unfamiliar territory in heavy traffic during a blizzard. If the storm hits New Hampshire on Saturday, that means I'll probably be running into it in Pennsylvania or New York. I'll have to decide whether to try to beat it home or wait until it passes through.

It hits me like a slap in the face. This will be the first time I'm ever coming home from a vacation and my mother will not be waiting to welcome me back. She would have been so proud of me for daring to take this trip. Oh, she would have hated to have me gone, but proud that I would do it. She'd love to hear the stories and see the pictures. It's going to be hard walking into that house and not hearing her greeting. Tears fall.

The indoor pool here uses mineral salts instead of chlorine and a good swim is just what I need. The water feels wonderful. My skin feels so much better. The woman at the desk says it's the latest thing. She also says that Fredericksburg has many great sites to visit and that adds to my dilemma of staying longer or trying to get home quick.

DAY 32, FEB. 21

A Stop in Scranton, Pa.

There are a lot of things to see in the city, but I'm worried about the storm back home. I'm afraid if I wait, I'll end up driving in bad weather. As much as I'm tempted to explore, I am heading for home. I leave Fredericksburg at 9:15 a.m. It's 35 degrees under bright sunny skies. I head north on Rte. 17 and once I get out of the city, I enjoy the drive.

The countryside is beautiful, though mostly bare trees and dried yellow fields this time of year. The farmlands are huge and there are miles of open county and rolling hills. For a long time, the traffic is sparse and I enjoy this driving. I hold up the camera with one hand and take pictures once in a while. I love the farms. They are unique and beautiful. Silos rise tall and some farms have two or three. There are red barns, white barns, and gray dilapidated barns and other outbuildings. Some of the homes are simple single story ranch houses and others look almost like plantation houses. I am impressed with fences, too, that run for miles and miles; black, wide board fences, shorter white fences, barbed wire fences and natural corral fences. There are massive trees that dot the hills and valleys, but no forests like we have in New Hampshire.

Although I would love to explore the Virginia coast and see Williamsburg, inland has its beauty, too. I want to come back during spring or fall sometime to see this state when it's in color. That also would be a better time to visit the historic sites. How much more interesting history is when I can actually visit the sites and get a physical feel for the countryside. It's not much fun when it's only 30 degrees and the frigid wind is blowing through my clothes. I pass by many wildlife refuges where on a warmer day, I would have gladly stopped.

Rte. 66W is reached at 10 a.m. and the speed limit is 70 mph as I head towards the Shenandoah River Valley and the mountains.

Heading Towards the Mountains

I get to Rte. 81N half an hour later and the speed limit drops to 65. There's heavy traffic in the Winchester area, but after awhile it spreads out. I cross into West Virginia at 11 a.m., Maryland at 11:25 and Pennsylvania ten minutes after that. It's 32 degrees and the odometer reads 16,498.7. I take a quick break at a rest stop. The wind is brutal.

At noon, I stop for lunch at a Perkins Family Restaurant in Chambersburg. They have specials for those of us over 55. I get gas at a Sheetz across the street for $3.59/gal. I take a few photos of a place that looks to be an old railroad station and I'm back on the highway at 1 p.m.

Pennsylvania has beautiful countryside, too. Along Rte. 81, the elevations are higher and steeper. The farmlands are just as impressive. I would love to get some horse photos. I also want to know more about the mining communities and see first-hand more of that territory. Cities still scare me and traffic gets more intense. The speed limits fluctuate between 55 and 65 and there are signs in some areas saying fines are doubled. I slow down nearer the limit and vehicles pass me on both sides.

Not all the sights are of beautiful farms or modern cities. There are the signs of industry. Are these remnants of old coal mines? Some are interesting, some ugly like sections of land ripped apart and abandoned with debris and black . . . I don't know. It leaves me with questions and wanting to know more.

I begin to see snow in the outlying areas just south of Harrisburg.

The highway climbs up and up. It seems to cut right into the sides of mountains and there are vast expanses of views . . . when I can grab a glimpse. Then there comes a section where it seems the highway is along a narrow ridge with steep drop-offs to either side, first on one side then the other. Sometimes the northbound lane is higher than the south and vice versa. The views must be amazing, kind of like the Skyline Drive only at 60 mph in heavy traffic, if I could take the time to look. It's a little nerve wracking. The road curves and rises and dips; long and winding, rising up and across then back down a long, curvy slow grade. I do chance a few driving photos, but it's scary to do so. This road would be horrendous during a storm.

Comin' 'Round the Mountain

I am getting tired and my concentration is slipping. I wriggle in the seat, taking turns shaking my hands and arms, and tapping on my thighs. My butt hurts from sitting so long. When I start weaving a little bit in the lane, I figure it's time to find a hotel. I really hadn't thought I'd make Scranton today, so I am pleased that I do after driving 319.9 miles for a total of 3,514.1. This Comfort Suites Inn is a little pricey. Ohhh, it's beside a ski resort; that must be why. They give me a senior discount on top of the AAA. I am checked in by 4 p.m. She gives me a room with the view of the ski area. It's all lit up at night.

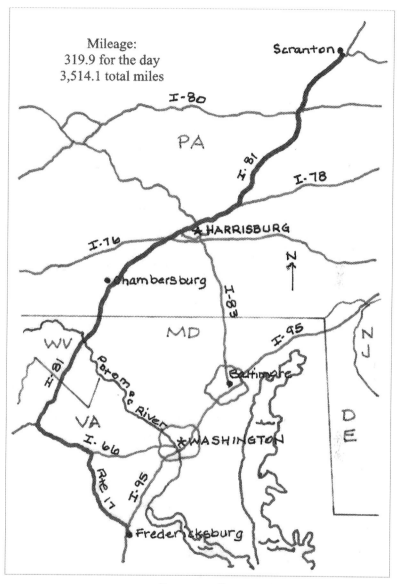

Mileage:
319.9 for the day
3,514.1 total miles

Scranton, Pa.

Bringing the luggage in is not easy. It's only 28 degrees and I don't even want to know what it is with the wind chill. The luggage trolley doesn't wheel right and I struggle. I finally settle in and debate about a swim, but figure it's more important to check in, write my blog, and order dinner. Tomorrow I'll have to work and watch the weather to see if I should stay longer or if I will have time to get closer to home.

DAY 33, FRIDAY, FEBRUARY 22

The Last Hotel

I've been up since 4:30 and at work by 5. This place is noisy and the first where I could hear snoring from the next room. I woke about 2 a.m. and couldn't get back to sleep; not because of the snoring, I just couldn't sleep. I check weather in New York and it doesn't show snow this morning. According to Google maps, the quickest and easiest way home is to take Rte. 84E into Connecticut and get on I-91N to Rte. 9 in Vermont. I could be home in six hours without any stops and in current driving conditions.

Wow, home. I want to be home and I don't. I don't want to come home to a storm, that's for sure. My emotions about returning are . . . scattered. I want to see my kitty, but to come home to that house and to snow and cold isn't something to look forward to. I should be glad to get home. It will be nice to sleep in my own bed and watch TV without having to deal with commercials. It will be nice to call people on a phone that works.

What's my life going to be when I get home? I'm not expecting any big revelations on this journey, but I want to feel different. I want to have some new energy, some spark. I've certainly enjoyed the traveling. I'm afraid I will just crash when I get in that house; the house that is mine because I own it, but it's not me. It's a house that holds sad memories.

Perhaps this means one decision will be made; the decision to sell. Of course, then I'll have to consider where to go. I like the area and I like my job. This is the first area I've ever lived where I have a community of friends and I feel I belong.

Well, I suppose if I start moving now and pack up, I can be on the road by 9 a.m.

Dashing for Home

The temperature at the hotel when I leave at 8:55 a.m. is 26 degrees. The odometer reads 16,680.2 and I have half a tank of gas. The sky is overcast. The lady at the desk never says goodbye, never asks how my stay was; she doesn't make any comment when I hand over the key. This wasn't a very welcoming place. As I drive out of Scranton and exit Rte. 81N onto Rte. 84E, the sky lightens and I see patches of blue. It's hard to tell if there's more blue or more clouds. It's bright enough that I put on my sunglasses.

The New York border is crossed and I enter the Hudson River Valley an hour later with the speed limit still 65 mph. An elevation sign at a high point reads 1,272 ft. For the most part, although there are beautiful farm lands, the drive is tedious, especially when the speed limit drops to 55. I slow down and vehicles pass on both sides. I feel sleepy and do my usual wriggling in the seat, shaking arms and hands, pounding on my legs, and shaking my head. It's scary catching myself dozing off. Still, the drive across New York doesn't take too long. I take a few photos as I drive and when I cross the Hudson River, paying a toll of $1.50, I find the battery dead in the camera. Drat, I want pictures of the bridge.

I stop in Fishkill at 10:30 a.m. to have a late breakfast at the Rte. 84 Diner. I change the battery in the camera and hobble inside where I order two eggs over hard with the yolks broken, two pancakes, bacon and orange juice for $10.45 counting the tip. I can't eat all the pancakes. It's 11:15 when I leave to go across the street to the Sunoco station for gas. Oh, my God! The price is $3.97/gal. and that's the cash price. I pay $30 and end up with three-quarters of a tank. What's going on with the gas prices?

I pass into Connecticut at 11:45 a.m., odometer reading 16,811.1 and it's 37 degrees. The speed limit is 65 and I want to drive faster. I allow myself 5 mph over the limit.

Getting Through Hartford, Ct.

Rte. 91N is reached an hour later, Massachusetts at 1:25 p.m. and Vermont at 1:55. I make a quick bathroom break at a rest stop, reach the New Hampshire border at 3:15 and arrive home about 3:45 p.m. The worst driving of the day was between Keene and Hillsborough. All my fears of getting caught in the storm were unfounded. I am home safe and sound (okay, maybe the sound could be questioned, ha ha.)

I am home after 33 days and driving 3,856.5 miles. The amazing adventure is over.

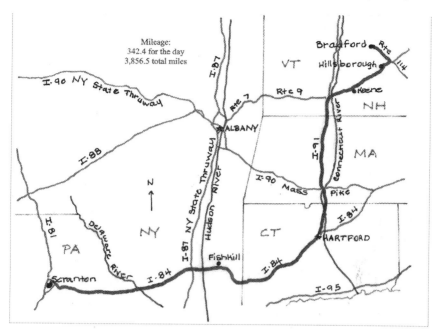

Home

Kitty, I'm Hoooomme!

Coming into Bradford, I am concerned about my emotions at arriving home and walking into the house for the first time in 33 days. How will it be to not have my mom greet me? Will I have an emotional breakdown? This would be my first time coming home from a vacation without her being here. Will Freyja come running when I holler my greeting? What if she pulls a typical cat thing and ignores me? I'm probably going to be an emotional wreck.

When I pull into the yard, Karen and her son, Evan are just arriving to tend to Freyja. I hadn't been specific when I'd return because the weather worries kept the trip spontaneous to the last minute. If I'd run into bad weather, I would have found a hotel for the night. It's a relief having them here and it forces me to hold myself together.

We go inside and I call to Freyja, "Kitty, I'm hoommme!" She doesn't come running like she does normally, but as Karen and I stand in the kitchen talking, kitty shows up looking as if she can't believe it's really me. I call, "Hi,

Kitty," and she runs to me. I scoop her up as tears fill my eyes. "I missed you so much," I whisper into her fur.

I dry my eyes and Karen and I continue catching up. I give her the sweet grass basket I bought for her in South Carolina. I cannot thank her enough for watching over things while I was away and to be here when I got home probably saved me from falling to pieces. Gosh, I'm getting to be an emotional old git.

After Karen and Evan leave, I do a quick check in to let everyone know I got back okay. I drag most everything in from the truck, then crash on the couch. The actual unpacking can wait until tomorrow.

Coming Home to a Storm

EPILOGUE

The Adventure Ends

Coming home; the finality, the ending of an adventure, the getting back to "normalcy" if ever one can. The excitement of the traveling and meeting new people fell away and the stories told to family and friends could only be repeated so much. The big revelation I was hoping for during the trip didn't happen. The goals of "finding myself" or figuring out my future did not jump out at me. I settled back down to a mostly stay-at-home existence with the companionship of my darling kitty; the same old same old. The only difference was that I had this book to write and hundreds of photos to edit and that was exciting.

Writing the Book

An adventure like this cannot be taken without having consequences and while some aspects were over, the journey was relived through turning the blog writings into a book. I poured back over those entries and all the notes written in various little notebooks and on loose pieces of paper. I had refused to use a mechanical recorder because part of the adventure was remembering. History and other information were researched on the internet along with what was gleaned from tour guides and story boards at sites to add extra pizzazz to the writing.

Months went by as obstacles and life struggles threatened to crush me. I plugged away at the writing and photo editing doing little other art work. Then in July, I was once more devastated with an immense loss when I had to put down my beloved kitty, Freyja. It was almost too much to bear. I knew if I didn't get another kitty that I would be forever lost and a few weeks later, Pele came into my life. She saved me.

When I got back into the book, new problems arose. Nothing is as easy as they make it sound. I didn't make it easy for myself as this project was not a simple writing, but a complex piece of work. I refused to bow down to the dictates of what others had done. I had a specific goal in mind. As a writer and a photographer, I not only wanted to "tell my story," but I wanted to "show you." The question filled me, "Why can't there be many pictures in a book?"

Although the first draft was written, there was still much to do. I realized my goal of providing color photos would be too costly for this size book. Microsoft Word kept freezing up on me and after receiving some advice, tried a different approach. By the end of August, I was starting from scratch in rebuilding the book; copying, pasting, and adjusting from the template in Microsoft Word to one in Open Office. There was a learning curve as Open Office didn't work exactly like MS Word. Plus, all the photographs needed to be changed to black and white and re-inserted. Some photos did not transfer well to grayscale and others needed to be used which meant more editing and making text changes to the List of Photos page.

And yet, through all the struggling, a new lease on life was taking hold. I'd been feeling guilty because I hurry from one place to another without fully taking the time for a deeper experience. It took months to realize that this is how I am and that I should be celebrating that aspect of myself. I live by the moment so it only stands to reason that my journeys should be the same way. They are moments. There's so much I want to see and do that I cannot spend a lot of time in one place. This IS who I am. This is how I work. Why not play to it?

The writing continued to improve and my style of writing began to stand out. Confidence grew and my focus became more intense. Here, months after my life-changing journey, I was finally getting it! Most revealing was finally coming to understand who I am as a writer.

I've come through terrible grief and loneliness and now I feel like I'm a new person. I've re-invented myself as a travel writer/photojournalist and have a goal in life; one that will take my entire life to experience and record. The ideas consume me and I'm bursting at the seams. Oh, I have a lot of books to write! I can't wait for the next adventure . . .

IN MEMORY OF FREYJA

Before I could get this book finished, I had to put my baby-kitty down. She had cancer and stopped eating. Was there a part of me that knew? While I journeyed south this past winter, was that why I worried about her so much? She was such a part of my emotional state. I missed her so much. Was my traveling the beginning of the letting go?

There is quite a story of how Freyja came to us. The day arrived when I was ready to get another cat, so on July 22, 1999, Ma and I went to the SPCA to get two kitties. My boyfriend at the time said he thought Maine coon cats were nice. Ma was adamant that we were NOT going to get a Maine coon cat just because Mike liked them. She kept repeating that statement until I snapped that no, I would not get that breed.

We were shown a room of cages. This kitty was in a cage by herself because she didn't like other cats. Every time we walked by looking over all the kitties, she'd reach out her paw to touch my mother's elbow and Ma would say, "I think this one is nice." None of the other kitties "spoke" to me and with the pleading eyes and that paw reaching out, we couldn't resist. She definitely did the choosing. We decided to forego getting two cats and adopt the one who so wanted to come home with us.

What a surprise to be filling out the paperwork when they wrote Maine coon cat for the breed. I laughed and said to Ma, "You're not going to believe this," and told her. Her only comment was, "Don't tell Margaret." (Margaret was my mother's twin and the three of us ladies lived together. They did not like Mike.)

The moment we let kitty out of the box, she was ours wholeheartedly. She didn't run and hide or go off to explore. She stayed right with me, following me around. I needed to come up with a name and the next day, I opened a book called "365 Goddesses." For the day's date, July 23, Freyja, the Norse goddess of love and devotion was listed. The text added that when sad, she'd cry tears of gold. At the time, kitty's eyes were more gold than green and she was so lovable. So Freyja she became.

From the start, Freyja was a phenomenal kitty. She had an almost perfect M on her forehead and I used to say that she was Ma's kitty, Margaret's kitty, and MY kitty. There was a loft above my bedroom and she would join me in my reading place at the top of the stairs. She'd share pieces of cheese steak subs although she was never a people-food cat. She took to walking the railings of the loft like a tight-rope and would leap down to my bed on the floor below. A flying kitty was an amazing sight to witness.

She was fascinated by the water cooler and the dishpan full of soapy water. She didn't want her water dish on the floor near her food dish. She knew the water came from the taps and wanted her water beside the sinks. We kept a dish next to each one because she also wanted water in the bathrooms.

She didn't play normal kitty games, either. She'd be up near the top of the stairs and I'd toss little balls to her. She'd bat them back at me. We played tag around the rooms. Even though I knew she was going to jump out at me, I'd squeal every time she did. We continued the game of tag when we moved to Barrington. I'd get down on my hands and knees around the kitchen island and couches and we'd sneak up on each other.

In Bradford, I laid a wide poster tube open on both ends on the floor that I got at Barnes & Noble and she loved hiding in the tunnel to jump out when I walked by. She could open closet doors to find places to sleep. I'd go upstairs to bed and discover my bureau drawers open with the clothes hanging out as she made sleeping places inside. She'd push the bathroom door open after I got out of the shower and brush up against my wet legs as I was drying off. She'd wait until I was dropping off to sleep at night then jump on the bed for kitty-pats.

We got older, she and I. I could no longer get on my hands and knees to crawl around. I put plastic tote bins near the counters to help her jump up. After I hurt my back, I piled couch cushions around me in the evening to watch TV. I'd lay my right arm across the pillow palm up and she'd straddle my arm so I could kitty-scratch her neck, chin, and belly. She had the softest fur.

Fourteen years is a good long life for a cat, almost 14 years to the day since she came into my life. But, she was ready to go. I could feel it in her body and see it in her face. On her last night, she was extra lovable and cuddly. She never allowed hugs, but this night she let me pick her up and hold her for a long time. She knew. She was saying her goodbyes.

The next morning, she didn't come to greet me and I knew. It took awhile to find her even though I called and called. She was in her kitty condo and looked out at me with sad eyes. It was heartbreaking. She was already leaving. I pulled her out and we took that last ride to the vets. I was with her to the end. It wasn't easy saying goodbye. I loved her so much. She was my comfort and my joy. She kept me from being alone. But I know I made the right decision. It was her time. She was done and she knew it.

It seems uncanny that the finishing of the first draft of this book was also the ending of her life; an ending to a part of my life. She will always be in my memory and have a special place in my heart. She was my "bestest best kitty" and I told her that all the time. She knew. I knew. Love you, Baby-kitty, Freyja. I miss you.

The Light in Her Eyes